Austin Powers: International Man of Mystery

Mike Kozarski

EXT. LAS VEGAS (STOCK FOTTAGE) - NIGHT
GRAPHIC: 1967 - SOMEWHERE IN NEVADA
It is set against the obvious skyline of Las Vegas.

INT. DR. EVIL'S PRIVATE QUARTERS - DAY
The lair is 1960's high-tech. We see a huge oversized conference table with six scary-looking EVIL ASSOCIATES, including a Latin American REVOLUTIONARY in a field jacket and turtleneck, TWIN NORDIC DOCTORS, and a METER MAID.

ANGLE ON: A RING WITH DR. EVIL'S INSIGNIA ON IT.
THE RINGED HAND IS STROKING A WHITE FLUFFY CAT.

DR. EVIL
(face always unseen)
Gentlemen, are we all here? Good.
As you know, my plot to high-jack nuclear weapons and hold the world hostage has failed. Again. This organization will not tolerate failure.
He presses a button. The Revolutionary, the twin Nordic doctors, and the meter maid's chairs tip back and fall into a pit. Their chairs return empty and smoking.

DR. EVIL
Mustafa...
ANGLE ON: MUSTAFA, an Arab with a red Fez.

DR. EVIL
Frau Farbissina...
ANGLE ON FRAU FARBISSINA in a severe Salvation Army uniform.

DR. EVIL
I spared your lives because I need you to help me rid the world of the only man who can stop me now. We must go to London. I've set a trap for Austin Powers!

EXT. CARNABY STREET - DAY
MUSIC: Soul Bossanova by QUINCY JONES.
We start on a pair of BEATLE BOOTS and peg-top crushed velvet pants walking down the street in rhythm, la Saturday Night Fever.
We pan up to reveal AUSTIN POWERS, International Man of Mystery. He's a swinger, with medium-length Mod hair and sideburns and he wears National Health Services glasses.
Austin walks along Carnaby Street taking photographs. It is that perpetual bright sunny day you see in Sixties movies.
Austin, bursting with life, gives a two-handed handshake to a MOD FREAK, who's just gotten off a red double-decker bus.

Austin salutes a strolling BOBBY, then comes across TWO
BEAUTIFUL MOD GIRLS who are excited to see him. They all start to twist to the music,
including the Bobby.

FREEZE FRAME - TECHNICOLOR BLUE TINT - TITLE CARD
**(PRODUCTION NOTE: ALL TITLE CARDS WILL BE DONE IN
TECHNICOLOR FREEZE FRAMES LA SWEET CHARITY.)**
In the middle of the street, THREE MODELS wait impatiently to be photographed in a
makeshift photo shoot arca.
One wears a short-skirted Stewardess outfit. One wears a metallic silver pantsuit with
matching cowl. The other wears a see-through Mary Quant dress.

AUSTIN
(taking photos)
Alright, luv! Love it! Turn...pout for me baby. Smashing!
We see that AUSTIN HAS VERY BAD ENGLISH TEETH. The model in the stewardess
outfit foes on all fours.

AUSTIN
Crazy baby. Give me some shoulder.
Yes! Yes! Yes!
(beat)
No. No.
Show me love. Yes! And...done. Here you go, luv. I'm spent.
Austin throws the camera in the air behind him. An ASSISTANT scrambles and catches it
before it hits the ground.

AUSTIN
Get these off to Fab Magazine right away.

SUPERMODEL 1
Austin, you've really outdone yourself this time.

AUSTIN
Thanks, baby.

SUPERMODEL 2
(suggestively)
We could have another photo session back at my flat.

AUSTIN
(coyly)
Oh, behave!

SUPERMODEL 3
Austin, I love you!

AUSTIN
So many women, so little time.
A gaggle of MOD GIRLS come towards the shoot site. They recognize Austin and SCREAM hysterically.

MOD GIRL 1
It's Austin Powers!
Austin runs away. The mob chases after him a la Hard Day's Night.

EXT. CARNABY STREET
Two BAD GUYS attack Austin. He JUDO CHOPS them.

AUSTIN
Judo chop! Judo chop!
The mob of girls catches up to Austin and he runs away.

EXT. PHONE BOOTH
Austin's in a phone booth with his back turned. The mob runs by. He steps out, disguised only by a beard.

EXT. GUARD STATION - LONDON - DAY
Austin is jiving down the street and comes across a stoned- face red-coated BUCKINGHAM PALAM GUARD standing at attention just outside his guard box.
Austin mugs for the guard, trying to get him to crack up, but to no avail. Finally, he pulls a big sixties FLOWER from behind the guard's head and presents it to him. They both crack up.

EXT. PHOTO BOOTH
The girls run by a Sixties-era photo booth with somebody inside. Austin steps out.

ANGLE ON THE FILM STRIP
Panels 1-3 show Austin with various exotic MODELS. The fourth panel shows Austin with the QUEEN.

EXT. CARNABY STREET
Austin spots a VERY PREGNANT HIPPY GIRL with a placard that says "PROTEST!" in a funky font.

AUSTIN

4

You might want to protest a bit louder next time, luv.
The both laugh.

2L FULL SCREEN INSERT - AUSTIN'S PASSPORT
The passport opens. We see Austin's dour photo. Then he gives an insane grin, showing his bad teeth. The page flips and we see visa stamps from all the exotic places he's been.

EXT. CARNABY STREET - DAY
Austin flips a coin into a BLIND MAN's cup. The blind man, obviously sighted, moves the cup to catch the coin. Austin wags his finger in a "oh, you" fashion, and then proceeds to knee him the balls.

EXT. CARNABY STREET - DAY
Austin is being chased around the corner by a GAGGLE OF

SCHOOLGIRLS.
After a moment, Austin returns from around the corner with a baton, followed by a MARCHING BAND.
The schoolgirls pick up his trail again and he begins to run.
A 1967 Jaguar XKE convertible, which is decorated with a large Union Jack, pulls beside Austin.
He jumps over the door into the moving convertible, racing off just ahead of the crowd.

EXT./INT. JAGUAR - STREETS OF LONDON - DAY
The driver of the Jag is Austin's associate, MRS. KENSINGTON, a beautiful woman in her thirties.
They drive against obvious REAR PROJECTION of 1960's London.

AUSTIN
Hello, Mrs. Kensington.

MRS. KENSINGTON
Hello, Austin Just then, a FLASHING
RED LIGHT goes off and we hear a distinctive PHONE RING.

MRS. KENSINGTON
That'll be Basil Exposition, Chief of British Intelligence.
The glove compartment revolves to reveal a picture phone.
ANGLE ON: PICTURE PHONE SCREEN. We see BASIL EXPOSITION a distinguished older man. A desk plate reads: "Basil Exposition, Chief of British Intelligence."

BASIL EXPOSITION
(on picture phone)

Hello, Austin. This is Basil Exposition, Chief of British Intelligence.
You're Austin Powers, International Man of Mystery, and you're with Agent Mrs. Kensington. The year is 1967, and you're talking on a picture phone.

AUSTIN
We know all that, Exposition.

BASIL EXPOSITION
I just wanted to be extremely clear so that everyone knows what's going on at any given time. We've just received word that Dr. Evil, the ultimate square, is planning to take over the world.

AUSTIN
Dr. Evil? I thought I put him in jail for good.

BASIL EXPOSITION
I'm afraid not. Earlier this week,
Dr. Evil escaped from Zedel Edel Prison in Baaden Baaden and now he's planning a trap for you tonight at the Electric Psychedelic Pussycat Swinger's Club in Picadilly Circus here in swinging London.
A panel revolves to reveal a map of London with lights showing Austin's position and the location of the club.

AUSTIN
Just where you'd never think to look for him. We'll be there.

BASIL EXPOSITION
Good luck, Austin.

AUSTIN
Thank you.

BASIL EXPOSITION
Oh, and Austin&emdash;

AUSTIN
Yes?

BASIL EXPOSITION
(pause)
Be careful.

AUSTIN

Thank you.
(to Mrs. Kensington)
Let's go, baby!

EXT. STOCK FOTTAGE - PICADILLY CIRCUS - NIGHT
On top of one building is a three-story high BOB'S BIG BOY figure.

EXT. ELECTRIC PSYCHEDELIC PUSSYCAT SWINGER'S CLUB - NIGHT
The Jaguar pulls up in front of the swinging nightclub.
Mrs. Kensington steps out of the car, dressed in a tight leather fightsuit. She looks fabulous.

INT. ELECTRIC PSYCHEDELIC PUSSYCAT SWINGER'S CLUB
It's a swinging club. FREAKS abound. In one corner, there is a PRESS CONFERENCE in progress.

MICK JAGGER
Hey Austin Powers, it's me, Mick Jagger.

AUSTIN
Hey, Mick!

MICK JAGGER
Are you more satisfied now sexually,
Austin?

AUSTIN
Well, you can't always get what you want.

MICK JAGGER
(thinking)
"You can't always get what you want!"
That's a great title for a song!
I'm gonna write that, and it'll be a big hit.

AUSTIN
Good on ya, man.

MICK JAGGER
Groovy!

FULL SCREEN INSERT
A vinyl 45 of "You Can't Always Get What You Want."

9 FULL SCREEN INSERT - BILLBOARD CHART
"You Can't Always Get What You Want" at Number One.

INT. ELECTRIC PSYCHEDELIC PUSSYCAT SWINGER'S CLUB
In one corner ANDY WARHOL sits in front of his multi-colored Elvis (or equivalent). He body paints a butterfly on the thigh of a MOD GIRL wearing a metallic miniskirt outfit.

ANDY WARHOL
Austin Powers? Hi, I'm Andy Warhol.

AUSTIN
Hey, how are you?

ANDY WARHOL
Hungry.

AUSTIN
Here, have this can of Campbell's Tomato Soup.
Austin hands Andy a can of soup.

ANDY WARHOL
I'm going to paint this can of soup and become famous and not give you any credit for it.

AUSTIN
If you can become famous, everyone will have their fifteen minutes of fame, man.

ANDY WARHOL
"Fifteen minutes of fame?" I'm going to use that quote and not give you any credit for that, either.

AUSTIN
Smashing!

FULL SCREEN INSERT
Andy Warhol's famous Soup Can painting.

INT. ELECTRIC PSYCHEDELIC PUSSYCAT SWINGER'S CLUB
HER MAJESTY, THE QUEEN is giving Austin a Victoria's Cross like the Lyndon Johnson scene in Forrest Gump. Behind them, are two COLDSTREAM GUARDS and the DUKE OF EDINBURGH.

QUEEN

Austin Powers, Britain owes you a debt of gratitude.
Austin gives a cheeky look to Mrs. Kensington.

QUEEN
I understand you were wounded. Where were you hit?

AUSTIN
In the but-tocks.

QUEEN
That must be a sight. I'd kind of like to see that.
Austin turns around, drops his pants, and shows his wounded bum (matching Gump's) to the queen.
The queen walks away.

QUEEN
(laughing)
Nice buttocks.
In the line-up we also see FOREST GUMP. He has to pee very badly.

MRS. KENSINGTON
We've got to find Dr. Evil!

AUSTIN
Wait, I've got an idea.
He PUNCHES a PRETTY MOD GIRL in the face, knocking her out cold.

EVERYONE
Ohhh!

MRS. KENSINGTON
Austin, why in God's name did you strike that woman?

AUSTIN
That ain't no woman! It's a man, man. It's one of Dr. Evil's assassins.
Austin pulls off the mod girl's wig. She is a MALE ASSASSIN.
The assassin comes to and leaps to his feet.
Mrs. Kensington knocks his feet from under him. The assassin hits the ground and pulls out a dagger. Mrs. Kensington kicks the knife out of his hand and Austin gets him in a head-lock from behind.

AUSTIN
Where's Doctor Evil?

ANGLE ON: A FINGER WITH DR. EVIL'S INSIGNIA ON IT.
THE FINGER PULLS THE TRIGGER OF A SPEAR GUN.
The assassin falls forward. A spear protrudes from his back. Austin sees Dr. Evil as he runs through a door.
They give chase.

INT. CLUB - BACK ROOM
They enter. Dr. Evil climbs into an egg chair.

AUSTIN
I've got you again, Dr. Evil!
The chair fills with a WHITE MIST.

DR. EVIL
(unseen, through mist)
Not this time. Come, Mr.
Bigglesworth!
(calling out)
See you in the future, Mr. Powers!
Before the doors close, the white CAT jumps in the egg chair.
A sign on the egg reads "CRYOGENIC

FREEZING BEGINNING."
MRS. KENSINGTON
My God! He's freezing himself.
Austin begins FIRING at the egg chair. The ceiling opens up and the egg rises through the opening. Everything begins to RUMBLE. Rocket exhaust pours out of the ceiling.

EXT. ROOF - NIGHT
The Bob's Big Boy rocket begins to LIFT OFF.

EXT. CLUB - SIDEWALK - NIGHT
PEOPLE outside the club react to the rocket.

EXT. EARTH FROM SPACE
The Bob's Big Boy rocket leaves the atmosphere. Mr.
Bigglesworth is pressed to the window like one of those stuffed Garfields.

DR. EVIL (V.O.)
(shivering)
I'll be back, Mr. Powers, when free love is dead, and greed and avarice once again rule the world.

EXT. NORAD - COLORADO SPRINGS, COLORADO
GRAPHIC: 1997 - NORAD - COLORADO SPRINGS THIS SCENE IS SHOT IN THE MULTIPLE SPLIT SCREEN STYLE, LIKE THE THOMAS CROWN AFFAIR:
16 FULL SCREEN - INT. NORAD TRACKING ROOM
A BLIP appears on the radar screen.

RADAR OPERATOR
(on phone)
Commander Gilmour?

17 SPLIT SCREEN 2 - INT. COMMANDER GILMOUR'S OFFICE
COMMANDER GILMOUR, a distinguished man in his fifties.

RADAR OPERATOR
(on phone)
Commander, this is Slater in SoWest Com Three. We have a potential bogey with erratic vectoring and an unorthodox entry angle.

COMMANDER GILMOUR
(on phone)
Is it one of ours?

RADAR OPERATOR
No. Log Com Bird Twelve says its metalurg recon analysis is a standard alloy, not stealthy, not carbon- composite.
(pause)
It does have an odd shape, sir.

COMMANDER GILMOUR
What are you saying, son?

RADAR OPERATOR
It appears to be in the shape of Bob's Big Boy, sir.

18 SCREEN 3 - THE BOB'S BIG BOY ROCKET
The rocket is dirty and battered from thirty years in space.

COMMANDER GILMOUR
Oh my God, he's back.

DRAMATIC STING

RADAR OPERATOR
In many ways, Bob's Big Boy never left, sir. He's always offered the same high quality meals at competitive prices.

COMMANDER GILMOUR
Shut up.

RADAR OPERATOR
Should we scramble TacHQ for an intercept?

COMMANDER GILMOUR
What's its current position?

19 SCREEN 4 - A RADAR MAP OF NEVADA
On the radar screen it says "NEVADA."

RADAR SCREEN
It was over Nevada, but...oh my God!
It's gone!

COMMANDER GILMOUR
Listen son, I want you to forget what you saw here tonight.

RADAR OPERATOR
Commander, I have to log it&emdash;

COMMANDER GILMOUR
That's a direct order. You didn't see a thing!
He hangs up and picks up another phone.

COMMANDER GILMOUR
(into phone)
Philips.

20 SCREEN 5 - SERGEANT PHILIPS AT HIS DESK
SERGEANT PHILIPS picks up the phone.

COMMANDER GILMOUR
Call the President

SCREEN 6 - THE WHITE HOUSE
COMMANDER GILMOUR
Prepare the jet...

22 SCREEN 7 - AN AIR FORCE JET ON A RUNWAY
COMMANDER GILMOUR
Get my overnight bag.

23 SCREEN 8 - AN OVERNIGHT BAG
COMMANDER GILMOUR
Philips, do me a favor and feed my fish.

SCREEN 9 - FISH IN A TANK
A hand enters and sprinkles fish food.

COMMANDER GILMOUR
Not too much!
The hand re-enters and scoops up some of the fish food.

COMMANDER GILMOUR
I'm going to London, England.

EXT. MINISTRY OF DEFENSE - LONDON, ENGLAND
GRAPHIC: LONDON, ENGLAND - MINISTRY OF DEFENSE MUSIC: "RULE BRITANNIA"
INT. M.O.D. - HALLWAY (OUTSIDE CRYOGENIC STORAGE FACILITY)
Basil Exposition (now aged 30 years), Command Gilmour, and NICOLAI BORSCHEVSKY, a Russian General, put on extreme-weather gear over their uniforms.

BASIL EXPOSITION
As you know, gentlemen, Dr. Evil had himself frozen in 1967. Soon after,
Austin Powers volunteered to have himself frozen, in the event Dr.
Evil should ever return. We believe Dr. Evil has begun yet another plot to take over the world. And that, gentlemen, is why we're here.

COMMAND GILMOUR
Outstanding re-cap, Exposition.
Command Gilmour opens a vault door. COLD MIST escapes.

INT. M.O.D. - CRYOGENIC STORAGE FACILITY
They pass a row of cryogenic holding berths, each containing a naked PERSON in suspended animation, a la Demolition Man.
They pass GARY COLEMAN, EVEL KNIEVAL (with cape), and VANILLA
ICE, all in suspended animation. They pass a now-empty berth with a plate that reads "JOHN

TRAVOLTA."
BORSCHEVSKY
Who is this Austin Powers? Is he a British operative?

BASIL EXPOSITION
No, he worked freelance, an internationally renowned swinging photographer by day and the ultimate gentlemen spy by night.
Finally, they come across Austin Powers: He is naked. His hands cover up his private parts. The look on his face suggests 'Oh my God, my bits and pieces are cold'. His glasses are frosted over. He is very hairy.

FEMALE ANNOUNCER
(on PA)
Attention, Stage One, laser cutting beginning.
Lasers begin to cut Austin out of the ice in one huge cube.

FEMALE ANNOUNCER
(on PA)
Laser cutting complete. Stage Two, warm liquid goo phase beginning.
A ROBOTIC ARM lifts the cube out of the berth and places it into a high-tech melting vat of warm liquid GOO.

FEMALE ANNOUNCER
(on PA)
Warm liquid goo phases complete.
Stage Three, reanimation beginning.
Austin comes to life out of the goo on a draining platform.

FEMALE ANNOUNCER
(on PA)
Reanimation complete. Stage Four, cleansing beginning.

INT. EXAMINATION AREA
Technicians lead a half-asleep Austin to a screened area, where only his feet and head are visible. He's washed off with a series of hot-water jets.

FEMALE ANNOUNCER
(on PA)
Cleansing complete. Stage Five, evacuation beginning.
He's given futuristic inoculations and then led to a screened- in toilet area. We can hear the sound of PEE ENTERING THE

BOWL.

He PEES for a while, then a little longer.
And then EVEN LONGER STILL.
The stream seems to be subsiding...then begins STRONGER than ever.
He is still PEEING.
Finally, it STOPS.

FEMALE ANNOUNCER (PA)
Evacuation com...
He begins PEEING again.
A little LONGER.
Then in short staccato BURSTS.
The it STOPS. Pause.
Two DRIPS.

FEMALE ANNOUNCER
Evacuation...
(waiting)
Complete! The cryogenic state of Austin Powers is now completed.
Austin lies in a bed tilted up in an extreme angle la Dr.
Frankenstein's lab. NURSE TECHNICIANS administer injections and monitor electrodes, IV's, and other biological sensors.

AUSTIN
(weakly)
Where am I?

BASIL EXPOSITION
You're in the Ministry of Defense.
It's 1997. You've been cryogenically frozen for thirty years.

AUSTIN
(shouting)

WHO ARE THESE PEOPLE?
BASIL EXPOSITION
The shouting is a temporary side- effect of the unfreezing process.

AUSTIN
Yes, I'm having trouble controlling&emdash;
(shouting)

THE VOLUME OF MY VOICE!
BASIL EXPOSITION

You might also experience a slight fever, dry mouth, and flatulence at moments of extreme relaxation.
Austin, this is Commander Gilmour,
Strategic Command, and General Borschevsky, Russian Intelligence.

AUSTIN
Russian Intelligence? Are you mad?

BASIL EXPOSITION
A lot's happened since you were frozen, Austin. The cold war's over.

AUSTIN
Thank God. Those capitalist dogs will finally pay for their crimes against the people, hey Comrades?

BASIL EXPOSITION
We won, Austin.

AUSTIN
Groovy. Smashing! Good on ya!
(to Gilmour)
Nice tie. Yea capitalism!

COMMANDER GILMOUR
Mr. Powers, the President's very concerned. We've got a madman on the loose in Nevada.

BASIL EXPOSITION
It's Dr. Evil.

AUSTIN
When do I begin?

BASIL EXPOSITION
Immediately. You'll be working with Ms. Kensington.

AUSTIN
You mean Mrs. Kensington?

BASIL EXPOSITION
No, Austin, Mrs. Kensington has long- since retired. Ms. Kensington is her daughter.
VANESSA KENSINGTON, Mrs. Kensington's daughter, beautiful, mid-Twenties, English, enters. She is wearing a very conservative, business pantsuit. Her hair is up and she wears glasses. Austin's breath is taken away.

She sets down a huge stack of files.

BASIL EXPOSITION
Vanessa's one of our top agents.

AUSTIN
(out loud, to himself)
My God, Vanessa's got a smashing body. I bet she shags like a minx.
How do I tell them that because of the unfreezing process, I have no inner monologue?
(pause)
I hope I didn't say that out loud just now.
There is an uncomfortable SILENCE.

VANESSA
Mr. Powers, my job is to acclimate you to the Nineties. You know, a lot's changed since 1967.

AUSTIN
Well, as long as people are still having promiscuous sex with many anonymous partners without protection, while at the same time experimenting with mind-expanding drugs in a consequence-free environment, I'll be sound as a pound.

VANESSA
My mother's told me all about you.

AUSTIN
If it's a lie, goddamn her. It it's the truth, goddamn me.
(pause)
God, I hope that's witty. How's your mum?

VANESSA
My mother's doing quite well, thank you very much.

BASIL EXPOSITION
Yes, well...Agent Kensington will get you set up. She's very dedicated.
Perhaps, a little too dedicated.
(aside to Austin)
She's got a bit of a bug up her ass.
Good luck, Austin, the world's depending on you.

AUSTIN
Thank you, Exposition.

BASIL EXPOSITION
Oh, and Austin&emdash;

AUSTIN
Yes?

BASIL EXPOSITION
Be careful.

AUSTIN
Thanks.
Basil exits.

INT. M.O.D. - QUARTERMASTER'S WINDOW
Austin and Vanessa wait at the window.

VANESSA
Let's gather your personal effects, shall we?
A CLERK brings out a locker-basket and reads off a list.

CLERK
(reading)
Danger Powers, personal effects.

AUSTIN
Actually, my name's Austin Powers.

CLERK
It says here, name Danger Powers.

AUSTIN
Danger's my middle name.

CLERK
OK, Austin Danger Powers: One blue crushed-velvet suit. One frilly lace cravat. One gold medallion with peace symbol. One pair of Italian shoes. One pair of tie-dyed socks, purple. One vinyl recording album: Tom Jones, Live at Las Vegas.
One Swedish-made penis enlarger pump.

AUSTIN
(embarrassed)
That's not mine.

CLERK
(reading)
One credit card receipt for Swedish- made penis enlarger pump, signed Austin Powers.

AUSTIN
I'm telling you, baby, that's not mine.

CLERK
(reading)
One warranty card for Swedish-made penis enlarger pump, filled out by Austin Powers.

AUSTIN
I don't even know what this is.
This sort of thing ain't my bag, baby.

CLERK
(reading)
One book: Swedish-Made Penis Enlarger Pumps and Me: This Sort of Thing Is My Bag, Baby, by Austin Powers.
The clerk shows the book to Austin, who is humiliated.

AUSTIN
OK, OK man, don't get heavy, I'll sign. Just to get things moving, baby.

VANESSA
Listen, Mr. Powers, I look forward to working with you, but do me a favor and stop calling me baby. You can address me as Agent Kensington.
We have to leave immediately. We've preserved your private jet just as you left it. It's waiting at Heathrow Airport.

AUSTIN
(excited)
My jumbo jet? Smashing baby.

EXT. PLANE TAKING OFF - DAY
We see a plane taking off in silhouette.

EXT. PLANE IN FLIGHT - DAY
A multi-colored psychedelic jumbo jet with Austin's logo on the tailpiece.

INT. PRIVATE PSYCHEDELIC JET
The inside looks like Hugh Heffner's jet&emdash; rust shag carpet, brown walls, and beads. Austin and Vanessa sit on beanbag chairs. Vanessa works on her lap top.

AUSTIN

Pretty groovy Jumbo Jet, eh? How does a hot chick like you end up working at the Ministry of Defense?

VANESSA

I went to Oxford and excelled in several subjects, but I ended up specializing in foreign languages.
I wanted to travel -- see the world.
In my last year I was accepted into the M.O.D. in the Cultural Studies sector. I thought I was off on an exciting career, but my job was to read everything printed in every country. It's very boring. My whole day is spent reading wedding announcements in Farsi. If I do well with this case, I finally get promoted to field operative...

AUSTIN

That's fascinating, Vanessa. Listen, why don't we go into the back and shag?

VANESSA

I beg your pardon?

AUSTIN

I've been frozen for thirty years, man, I want to see if my bits and pieces are still working.

VANESSA

Excuse me?

AUSTIN

My wedding tackle.

VANESSA

I'm sorry?

AUSTIN

My meat and two veg.

VANESSA

Mr. Powers, please. I know that you must be a little confused, but we have a very serious situation at hand. I would appreciate it if you'd concentrate on our mission and give your libido a rest.

AUSTIN

Have you ever made love to a Chigro?

VANESSA
A Chigro?

AUSTIN
You know, a Chigro&emdash; part Chinese, part Negro&emdash; Chigro.

VANESSA
(offended)
We don't use the term 'Negro' anymore.
It's considered offensive.

AUSTIN
That's right. You're supposed to say 'colored' now, right?
(spotting the flight attendants)
Here's the stewardesses! Bring on the sexy stews!
The STEWARDESSES enter. They're not dressed very sexily.
One of them is a man and another wears braces.

FLIGHT ATTENDANT
Excuse me, did you say 'stewardess'?
We're called 'flight attendants' now, thank you very much.

AUSTIN
Oh, I get it, it's like 'I'm not a whore, I'm a sex worker', baby.

FLIGHT ATTENDANT
My name is Mrs. Wilkenson. There are a few things we need to discuss.
First of all, we're not wearing these.
She holds up some skimpy, lingerie-type flight outfits.

FLIGHT ATTENDANT
**ALSO, I HAVE SOME QUESTIONS ABOUT THE ITINERARY. IT SAYS
HERE, '4:30 - DINNER, 5:30 -**
Everyone Gets Naked and Covered with Baby Oil, 6:00 - Orgy'?

AUSTIN
Seems pretty straightforward, don't you think...listen darling, I think you're a fabulous bird.
Can I get your telephone number?

FLGHT ATTENDANT
(mock sexy)
Sure, it's easy to remember.
(writing on his hand)

It's 777-FILM. We have to prepare the craft for take-off now.

AUSTIN
Smashing! When we land I'll give you a tinkle on the telling bone.
The flight attendant gives him a chilly stare and then exits.

AUSTIN
Brrrr! She must be frigid. There's two things I know about life: one,
Americans will never take to soccer.
Two, Swedish girls and stewardesses love to shag!
They're shag-mad, man! Let me ask you a question, Vanessa, and be honest.

VANESSA
Sure.

AUSTIN
Do I make you horny?

VANESSA
What?

AUSTIN
Do I make you horny? Randy, you know. To you, am I eros manifest?

VANESSA
I hope this is part of the unfreezing process.

AUSTIN
Listen, Vanessa, I'm a swinger&emdash; that's what I do, I swing.

VANESSA
I understand that, Mr. Powers, but let me be perfectly clear with you, perhaps to the point of being insulting. I will never have sex with you, ever. If you were the last man on Earth and I was the last woman on Earth, and the future of the human race depended on our having sex simply for procreation, I still would not have sex with you.
Austin is oblivious.

AUSTIN
What's you point, Vanessa?

EXT. PLANE IN FLIGHT - NIGHT
Austin's plane. Time has passed.

IINT. PRIVATE JET - NIGHT
Vanessa's lap-top BEEPS.

COMPUTER VOICE
You've got mail!
ANGLE ON: the computer screen. It's Basil Exposition.

BASIL EXPOSITION
IIcllo Austin. IIcllo Vancssa. This is Basil Exposition, from British Intelligence.
There's a company in Las Vegas called Virtucon that we think may be linked to Dr. Evil.
Many of the Virtucon executives gamble at the hotel/casino where you'll be staying. That's
the first place you should look. Well, I'm off to the chat rooms.

AUSTIN
Thank you, Exposition.

BASIL EXPOSITION
Oh, and Austin&emdash;

AUSTIN
Yes?

BASIL EXPOSITION
Be careful.
Vanessa closes her lap-top.

PILOT
(over loudspeaker)
Ladies and gentlemen, we're beginning our final descent into Las Vegas International
Airport. Flight attendants will be coming by to collect your drinks, and I'll ask you at this
time to please return to the main cabin and put your bean-bags in the upright position.
Austin and Vanessa fasten the seatbelts on their bean bags.

EXT. AIRPLANE LANDING - NIGHT
We see a plane's lights landing at night.

ZOOM CUT TO:
INT. PSYCHEDELIC SCENE BREAK
MUSIC: Psychedelic Wa-wa Pedal Funky Drummer Beat TITLE
GRAPHIC: The Trip Using a sequence of snap-zooms, colored projections, and flashing
lights, we see Austin dance crazily
la BOB FOSSE with a GO-GO GIRL in a bikini with the Austin Powers logo body-painted
on her midriff.

The sequence lasts five seconds and is very groovy.

EXT. LAS VEGAS MONTAGE - NIGHT
Sights and sounds of Las Vegas icons at night: "Welcome to Las Vegas" sign. Luxor. The giant cowboy whose arm waves.
Caesar's Palace. The montage ends on the modern skyline of Las Vegas.

GRAPHIC: 1997, SOMEWHERE IN NEVADA
INT. DR. EVIL'S PRIVATE QUARTERS
DR. EVIL
(face again unseen)
Ladies and Gentlemen, it's been a long time, but I'm back. It's all gone perfectly to plan except for one small flaw. Because of a technical error, my right arm was not frozen. I was therefore by definition only partially frozen.
ANGLE ON EVIL ASSOCIATE MUSTAFA. He is terrified and sweaty, eyes darting left and right.

MUSTAFA
But my design was perfect! Your autonomic functions were shut down, and even though your arm wasn't frozen, the aging was retarded, therefore your right arm is only slightly older than the left.

DR. EVIL
Can't you see I'm only half a man?
Look at me, I'm a freak!
He holds up his older right arm, which looks normal.

MUSTAFA
But Dr. Evil, all you need to do is&emdash;
(holding up tennis ball)
--work with this tennis ball. Squeeze it for twenty minutes a day. A few months of that and it'll be just as strong as the other arm...

DR. EVIL
And look what you've done to Mr.
Bigglesworth!

ANGLE ON MR. BIGGLESWORTH who is now totally hairless, with a fringe of white hair around it's ears, like Dr. Evil himself.

MUSTAFA
We could not anticipate feline complications due to the reanimation process&emdash;

DR. EVIL
(face unseen)
Silence!

ANGLE ON A HAND WITH DR. EVIL'S RING ON IT
Dr. Evil presses a button. Mustafa's chair tips back and he falls backwards into a pit.

MUSTAFA
(blood-curdling scream)
Ahhhhhhhhh!

DR. EVIL
(face unseen)
Let this be a reminder to you all that this organization will not tolerate failure.

MUSTAFA'S SCREAMS ECHO FAINTLY ANGLE ON: DR. EVIL FOR THE FIRST TIME.
HE IS IN HIS EARLY FIFTIES AND IS BALD, WITH A HIDEOUS SCAR ON HIS CHEEK.

DR. EVIL
Gentlemen, let's get down to business.
More muffled SCREAMS.

DR. EVIL
We've got a lot of work to do.

MUSTAFA (O.S.)
(muffled)
Someone help me! I'm still alive, only I'm very badly burned.

DR. EVIL
(slightly distracted)
Some of you I know, some of you I'm meeting for the first time.

MUSTAFA (O.S.)
(muffled)
Hello up there! Anyone! Can someone call an ambulance? I'm in quite a lot of pain.

DR. EVIL
(very frustrated)
You've all been gathered here to form my Evil Cabinet. Excuse me.
He picks up a white phone and MURMURS into it.

25

MUSTAFA (O.S.)
(muffled)
If somebody can open the retrieval hatch down here, I could get out.
See, I designed this device myself and...oh, hi! Good, I'm glad you found me. Listen, I'm very badly burned, so if you could just&emdash;
SFX: Muffled Gunshot

MUSTAFA (O.S.)
(muffled)
Ow! You shot me!

DR. EVIL
Right. Okay. Moving on.

MUSTAFA (O.S.)
(muffled)
You shot me right in the arm! Why did&emdash; SFX: Muffled Gunshot.
Dr. Evil waits. Nothing.

DR. EVIL
Let me go around the table and introduce everyone. Frau Farbissina...

ANGLE ON FRAU FARBISSINA
DR. EVIL
...founder of the militant wing of the Salvation Army. Random Task...
RANDOM TASK is a large Korean man in a butler's uniform.

DR. EVIL
...a Korean ex-wrestler, evil handyman extraordinaire. Show them what you do.
He stands up, bows, then takes off his shoe and THROWS it.
It knocks the head off a sculpture across the room.

DR. EVIL
Thank you, Random Task. Patty O'Brien...
PATTY O'BRIEN, a small, wiry Irishman with fiery eyes.

DR. EVIL
...ex-Irish assassin. His trademark?
Around PATTY O'BRIENS WRIST is a charm bracelet.

DR. EVIL

A superstitious man, he leaves a tiny keepsake on every victim he kills. Scotland Yard would love to get their hands on that piece of evidence.

PATTY O'BRIEN
(heavy Irish accent)
Yes, they're always after me lucky charms!
Everyone in the room tries to keep a straight face.

PATTY O'BRIEN
What? What? Why does everyone always laugh when I say that? They are after me lucky charms.
They cannot contain their LAUGHTER.

PATTY O'BRIEN
(angry)
What?

FRAU FARBISSINA
(through suppressed laughter)
It's a television commercial with this little cartoon Leprechaun who is a benevolent imp who is very concerned that these children will steal his lucky charms which are foodstuffs fashioned into various shapes&emdash; hearts, moons, clovers, what have you...
(pause)
It's a long story.

DR. EVIL
Finally, I come to my number two man. His name: Number Two.
NUMBER TWO, a good-looking 40-year-old man with an eye-patch.

DR. EVIL
For thirty years, Number Two has run Virtucon, the legitimate face of my evil empire.
He hits a button. The conference table slowly rotates to reveal a large, illuminated map of the United States dotted by various miniature models.

NUMBER TWO
Over the last thirty years, Virtucon has grown by leaps and bounds. About fifteen years ago, we changed from volatile chemicals to the communication industry. We own cable companies in thirty-eight states.
The thirty-eight states illuminate on the map.

NUMBER TWO
In addition to our cable holdings, we own a steel mill in Cleveland.
A steel mill miniature illuminates in Cleveland.

NUMBER TWO
Shipping in Texas.
A ship off the coast of Texas illuminates.

NUMBER TWO
Oil refineries in Seattle.
An oil refinery illuminates in Seattle.

NUMBER TWO
And a factory in Chicago that makes miniature models of factories.
The miniature model factory lights up in Chicago.

NUMBER TWO
We also own the Franklin mint, which makes decorative hand-painted theme plates for collectors.
(holds up plate)
Some plates, like the Gone With The Wind series, have gone up in value as much as two-hundred and forty percent, but, as with any investment, there is some risk involved.

DR. EVIL
Gentlemen, I have a plan. It's called blackmail. The Royal Family of Britain are the wealthiest landowners in the world. Either the Royal Family pays us an exorbitant amount of money, or we make it look like Prince Charles, the heir to the throne, has had an affair outside of marriage and, therefore, they would have to divorce.
There is an uncomfortable silence.

NUMBER TWO
Um, Dr. Evil, Prince Charles did have an affair. He admitted it, and they are now divorced, actually.

DR. EVIL
People have to tell me these things.
I've been frozen for thirty years, throw me a bone here.
(pausing)
OK, no problem. Here's my second plan. Back in the Sixties I had a weather changing machine that was in essence a sophisticated heat beam which we called a "laser." Using this laser, we punch a hole in the protective layer around the Earth, which we scientists call the "Ozone Layer." Slowly but surely, ultraviolet rays would pour in, increasing the risk of skin cancer. That is, unless the world pays us a hefty ransom.
There is another uncomfortable silence.

NUMBER TWO

Umm, that also has already happened.

DR. EVIL
Right.
(pause)
Oh, hell, let's just do what we always do. Let's hijack some nuclear weapons and hold the world hostage.
(pause)
Gentlemen, it's come to my attention that a breakaway Russian Republic called Kreplachistan will be transferring a nuclear warhead to the United Nations in a few days. Here's the plan. We get the warhead, and we hold the world ransom...
(dramatic pause)

...FOR ONE MILLION DOLLARS!
There is an uncomfortable pause.

NUMBER TWO
Don't you think we should ask for more than a million dollars? A million dollars isn't that much money these days.

DR. EVIL
All right then...
(dramatic pause)

...FIVE MILLION DOLLARS!
There is another uncomfortable pause.

NUMBER TWO
Virtucon alone makes over nine billion dollars a year.

DR. EVIL
(pleasantly surprised)
Oh, really?
(slightly irritated)
One-hundred billion dollars.
(pause)
OK, make it happen. Anything else?

FRAU FARBISSINA
Remember when we froze your semen, you said that if it looked like you weren't coming back to try and make you a son so that a part of you would live forever?

DR. EVIL

Yes.

FRAU FARBISSINA
Well, after a few years, we got sort of impatient. Dr. Evil, I want you to meet your son.

DR. EVIL
My son?

FRAU FARBISSINA
Yes.
(calling out)
Scott!
SCOTT EVIL walks out. He is fifteen, grungy, and wears a Kurt Cobain T-shirt.

SCOTT EVIL
Hi.

DR. EVIL
Hello, Scott. I'm your father, Dr.
Evil.
(emotional)
I have a son! I have a son!
Everyone, I have a son!
(gesturing to globe)
Someday, Scott, this will all be yours.

SCOTT EVIL
I haven't seen you my whole life and now you show up and want a relationship? I hate you!

EXT. JAGUAR - DRIVING - VEGAS - DAY
Vanessa and Austin drive in his perfectly-preserved Jag.

AUSTIN
You've preserved my Jag! Smashing!

VANESSA
Yes, we've had it retrofitted with a secure cellular phone, an on-board computer, and a Global Geosynchronous Positioning Device. Oh, and finally, this.
The glove compartment revolves to reveal a display of various dental hygiene products&emdash; floss, toothpaste, toothbrush, dental mirror, and cleaning tool.

AUSTIN

Let me guess. The floss is garotte wire, the toothpaste contains plastic explosives, and the toothbrush is the detonation device.

VANESSA
No, actually. I don't know how to put this really. Well, there have been fabulous advances in the field of dentistry.

AUSTIN
Why? What's wrong with my teeth?

EXT. VEGAS HOTEL - NIGHT
The Union Jack-emblazoned Jaguar pulls up to the front door.

INT. VEGAS HOTEL ROOM
Vanessa carries her compact flight attendant bag and Austin takes his two bright red oversized leatherette Samsonite suitcases.

AUSITN
Which side of the bed do you want?

VANESSA
You're going to sleep on the sofa.
I'd like to remind you, Mr. Powers, that the only reason we're sharing a room is to support our cover story that we're a married couple on vacation.

AUSTIN
So, shall we shag now, or shall we shag later? How do you like to do it? Do you like to wash up first?
Top and tails? A whore's bath?
Personally, before I'm on the job, I like to give my undercarriage a bit of a how's-your-father.

AUSTIN
(off her angry reaction)
I'm just joking, Vanessa. Trying to get a rise out of you.
They both laugh.

VANESSA
Let's unpack.
HER LUGGAGE: In the inside flap is a types list of contents.
All of her items are in separate, labeled plastic bags.

AUSTIN

Gor blimey, nerd alert.

HIS LUGGAGE: He pulls out a Nehru jacket and a huge Remington shaver with huge English plug.

HER LUGGAGE: She pulls out a compact clothes steamer/travel iron and a Braun blow drier.

HIS LUGGAGE: He pulls out a vintage 1967 Playboy and a bottle of Jurgens lotion.

HER LUGGAGE: She pulls out Wet-Naps, her underthings in a plastic baggie marked "Underthings" and her shoes in a baggie marked "Shoes."

HIS LUGGAGE: He pulls out a miniature meditation gong and Hai Karate cologne.

HER LUGGAGE: She pulls out a dossier labeled "Dr. Evil -
Top Secret."

HIS LUGGAGE: He pulls out the Swedish penis enlarger pump.

Vanessa sees it.

AUSTIN
Hey, who put this in here? Someone's playing a prank on me! Honestly, this isn't mine.

VANESSA
(suffering)
I'm sure.

AUSTIN
I think I'll give that stew a ding-a- ling.
Austin casually dials the phone while looking at his palm.
After a beat we hear a loud MALE VOICE coming through the handset.

MOVIE PHONE VOICE
(through handset)
Hello! And welcome to 777-FILM!
Austin covers the mouthpiece and whispers to Vanessa.

AUSTIN
I got her answering machine.

INT. CASINO
Austin and Vanessa walk through the casino. Austin gives PEOPLE two-handed handshakes. They stare like he's a freak.

AUSTIN
I love Las Vegas, man. Oh, I forgot my x-ray glasses.

VANESSA
Here, use mine.

AUSTIN
I'm going to use a cover name. It's important that it be a generic name so that we don't draw attention to ourselves.

INT. CASINO
Austin and Vanessa join the high-rollers table. Number Two is there, complete with eyepatch. On one side of him is a beautiful ITALIAN WOMAN (a la SOPHIA LOREN) in a white dress with a white kerchief on her head. On the other side of him is an extremely large-breasted BIMBO.

AUSTIN
Do you mind if I join you?

NUMBER TWO
Not at all.
The DEALER deals.

DEALER
Seventeen.
Zoom in on Number Two's eyepatch.

NUMBER TWO'S MONOCULAR POV
GRAPHIC: "X-RAY EYEPATCH". We see everyone at the casino in their underwear. He looks at the next card in the shoe.
It is a 4.

NUMBER TWO
Hit me.

DEALER
You have seventeen, sir. The book says not to, sir.

NUMBER TWO
I like to live dangerously.
The dealer draws a card from the card shoe.

DEALER
Four. Twenty-one.
Everyone at the table applauds. The dealer deals to Austin and Number Two.

DEALER
(to Austin)

Eighteen.
(to Number Two)
Sixteen.

NUMBER TWO'S POV
GRAPHIC: "X-RAY EYEPATCH". He looks at the shoe at the shoe and sees that the next card is a ten.

NUMBER TWO
I'll stay.

DEALER
(to Austin)
Sir?
Smugly, Austin puts on Vanessa's x-ray glasses.

AUSTIN'S POV
GRAPHIC: "X-RAY SPECS". Everyone is in their underwear, but it is completely blurry.

DEALER
(to Austin)
Sir?

VANESSA
(quietly)
What's wrong?

AUSTIN
(quietly, to Vanessa)
I can't see a bloody thing.

VANESSA
Oh, I forgot to tell you, they're prescription X-ray glasses. I have very bad astigmatism.

DEALER
Sir, the table is waiting.

AUSTIN
(panicking)
Uh, hit me.
The table MURMURS.

DEALER

On an eighteen, sir?

AUSTIN
Yes, I also like to live dangerously.
The dealer deals him the ten.

NUMBER TWO
You're very brave.

AUSTIN
Cards are not my bag, man. Allow myself to introduce...myself. My name is Ritchie Cunningham.
Vanessa is mortified.

AUSTIN
(indicating Vanessa)
This is my wife, Enid.

NUMBER TWO
My name is Number Two.
He extends his hand to shake. Austin extends his hand, but misses and begins to shake the bimbo's breast. There is an awkward pause. Austin takes off his glasses.

VANESSA
(rescuing him)
Number Two? That's an unusual name.

NUMBER TWO
My parents were hippies.
(indicating Italian woman)
This is my Italian confidential secretary.

ITALIAN WOMAN
(Italian accent)
My name is Alotta
(quickly)
Alotta Fagina.

AUSTIN
I'm sorry, I'm just not getting it.
It sounds like you're saying your name is a lot of...never mind.
Listen, cats, I'm going to crash.
It's been a gas.

NUMBER TWO
Bye-bye, Mr...Cunningham?

AUSTIN
Peace, baby.
Austin and Vanessa leave.

INT. CASINO
VANESSA
Why did you leave so soon?

AUSTIN
That cat Number Two has an X-ray eyepatch. I get bad vibes from him, man. Listen, we should go back to the room, but first I have to go to the naughty chair and see a man about a dog.
He heads to the rest room.

INT. HIGH ROLLERS TABLE - CASINO
Number Two has been watching them. He presses a BUTTON.

INT. BATHROOM - CASINO
Austin enters to see a gregarious TEXAN in a huge cowboy hat. Austin enters a stall. The Texan enters the adjoining stall.

TEXAN
Good luck, buddy. You don't buy food, you rent it.

AUSTIN
Too right, youth.

INT. BATHROOM STALL
Austin sits down. Behind him, a panel SLIDES OPEN, revealing Patty O'Brien. His charm bracelet JINGLES. Austin looks back. Patty's bracelet is now garotte wire. He wraps it around Austin's throat. Austin gets his thumbs between the wire and certain death.

AUSTIN
(grunting)
Uh, uh!

INT. TEXAN'S STALL
The Texan can only see Austin's feet, which are moving about frantically. He can hear the

GRUNTING.
TEXAN
Hey pardner, just relax, don't force it! Use some creative visualization.

INT. AUSTIN'S STALL
Austin GRUNTS and snaps his head back into Patty O'Brien's crotch. Patty O'Brien GROANS in agony.

PATTY O'BRIEN
(groaning)
Ughhhhh...
Austin breaks free of the charm bracelet/garotte, grabs Patty O'Brien's head, and pulls it between his legs so that it hovers above the toilet bowl.

AUSTIN
Who does Number Two work for?

INT. TEXAN'S STALL
TEXAN
That's right! Show that turd who's boss!

INT. AUSITN'S STALL
AUSTIN
Who does Number Two work for?

PATTY O'BRIEN
(quietly, straining)
Go to hell.
Austin drops Patty's head into the toilet and FLUSHES. We hear MUFFLED GURGLING SOUNDS from Patty O'Brien.

INT. TEXAN'S STALL
The Texan hears all of this, and is now concerned.

INT. AUSTIN'S STALL
Austin reaches into Patty O'Brien's wallet. We see his Dr.
Evil ID card and Alotta's Virtucon business card with her address.

INT. BATHROOM
Austin is leaving his stall. The Texan can see Patty O'Brien's dead body head-first in the toilet.

TEXAN

37

Jesus Christ, what did you eat?

ANGLE ON THE FLOOR OF AUSTIN'S STALL
Patty O'Brien's lifeless hand hits the floor. The charms come tumbling out: a heart, a moon, a star, and a clover. A second later, a blue diamond falls out.

INT. PSYCHEDELIC SCENE BREAK
MUSIC: Psychedelic Wa-wa Pedal Funky Drummer Beat TITLE
GRAPHIC: Love Power Austin and the go-go girl dance crazily.

EXT. VEGAS HOTEL - MORNING
INT. HOTEL SUITE - DAY
Vanessa is on the phone on the bed sifting through photos and files on Dr. Evil, Virtucon, etc.
In the background, through an open door, we see that Austin is asleep on the couch.

VANESSA
(into phone)
Hello Mum?

INT. MRS. KENSINGTON'S HOUSE - LONDON
An older Mrs. Kensington sits in her suburban English front room.

MRS. KENSINGTON
(on phone)
Oh, hello Vanessa. How was the flight?

VANESSA (V.O.)
Great.

MRS. KENSINGTON
How's Austin?

VANESSA (V.O.)
He's asleep.

MRS. KENSINGTON
You didn't...

INT. HOTEL SUITE
VANESSA
Oh, God no, I made him sleep on the couch.

In the background, we see Austin get off the couch. He is very naked and very hairy. A strategically placed vase of flowers blocks his naughty bits from view.

MRS. KENSINGTON (V.O.)
I'm proud of you.

VANESSA
Why?

MRS. KENSINGTON (V.O.)
Because you managed to resist Austin Power's charms.
Austin moves towards the bathroom away from the flowers.
Right in the nick of time, Vanessa holds up a photo of Number Two and looks at it, blocking his naughty parts.

VANESSA
Well, God knows he tried, but I've been rather firm with him, Mummy.
You didn't tell me he was so obsessed with sex. It's bizarre.

MRS. KENSINGTON (V.O.)
You can't judge him by modern standards. He's very much a product of his times. In my day he could have any woman he wanted.

VANESSA
What about his teeth?

SPLIT SCREEN - HOTEL ROOM/MRS. KENSINGTON'S HOUSE
MRS. KENSINGTON
You have to understand, in Britain in the Sixties you could be a sex symbol and still have bad teeth. It didn't matter.

VANESSA
I just don't see it.

MRS. KENSINGTON
Just wait. Once Austin gets you in his charms, it's impossible to get out.

VANESSA
Did you ever...

MRS. KENSINGTON
Of course not. I was married to your father.

VANESSA
Did you ever want to?

MRS. KENSINGTON
Austin is very charming, very debonair. He's handsome, witty, has a knowledge of fine wines, sophisticated, a world-renowned photographer. Women want hin, men want to be him. He's a lover of love&emdash; every bit an International Man of Mystery.
We hear the TOILET FLUSH. Mrs. Kensington WIPES off the screen.
Austin re-enters from left to right, still NAKED. Vanessa holds up Austin's Fab Magazine shoot from the Sixties, and in perfect timing blocks his crotch from the camera.

VANESSA
You didn't answer my question, Mum.

MRS. KENSINGTON (V.O.)
I know. Let me just say this: Austin was the most loyal and caring friend I ever had.
I will always love him.

AUSTIN (V.O.)
Good morning, luv, who are you on the phone with?

VANESSA
(to her mother)
Do you want to talk to him?

MRS. KENSINGTON (V.O.)
No, it's been too long. Best to leave things alone.

VANESSA
(to Austin)
I'm on with a friend!
(to her mother)
Look, I'd better go. I love you.

MRS. KENSINGTON (V.O.)
I love you, Vanessa.
Vanessa hangs up. Austin enters wearing an "Austin Powers" robe.

AUSTIN
Good morning, Vanessa! I hope you have on clean underwear.

VANESSA
Why?

AUSTIN
We've got a doctor's appointment&emdash; an evil doctor's appointment.

EXT. VIRTUCON MAIN ENTRANCE - DRIVEWAY - DAY
THROUGH BINOCULAR POV CUT-OUTS
We see a black limousine pull up in front. Random Task and another BODYGUARD exit the limo and secure the area.

EXT. LAS VEGAS - BUSHES
We see that the binoculars belong to Vanessa. She and Austin are on a stakeout. Austin's Jag is in the background.

VANESSA
A limousine has just pulled up.

AUSTIN
Let me see.
Austin pulls into frame an extremely long telephoto lens attached to his vintage camera.

EXT. VIRTUCON MAIN ENTRANCE
TELEPHOTO LENS POV
Two more BODYGUARDS leave the building and approach the limo.
Number Two exits the building holding Mr. Bigglesworth, the hairless cat. He's not happy about this, and has a scratch on his cheek.
FREEZE FRAME. SFX: Camera motor drive.

EXT. BUSHES
AUSTIN
Hello, hello. That's Dr. Evil's cat.

VANESSA
How do you know?

AUSTIN
I never forget a pussy...cat.

EXT. FRONT ENTRANCE
TELEPHOTO LENS POV
Number Two hands the hairless cat through limo's window.
FREEZE FRAME. SFX: Camera motor drive.
The limousine speeds off.

EXT. BUSHES
VANESSA
Let's go get him!

AUSTIN
He's too well-protected right now.

VANESSA
We can't just sit here, Austin.

AUSTIN
Let me tell you a story. There's these two bulls on top of a hill checking out some foxy cows in the meadow below. The young bull says,
'hey, why don't we run down the hill and shag us a cow?', and the wise old bull replies, 'no, why don't we walk down the hill and shag all the cows?'

VANESSA
I don't get it.

AUSTIN
Well, you know...cows, and shagging.

VANESSA
Unfortunately, while you told that stupid story, Dr. Evil has escaped.

AUSTIN
No worries, luv. We'll just give Basil a tinkle on the telling bone...
He notices the way the desert light catches her beauty.

AUSTIN
My God, Vanessa, you are so incredibly beautiful. Stay right where you are.
Austin changes lenses and begins SNAPPING PICTURES.

VANESSA
I hate having my picture taken.

AUSTIN
You're crazy. The camera loves you,
Vanessa.
Vanessa does a few coy poses.

AUSTIN
Go, Vanessa, go!

Vanessa lets go a little bit more.

WHITE CYC
Austin and Vanessa are in the midst of a full professional photo shoot, and she's loving it. Austin begins SNAPPING pictures, all the while changing her look, touching her hair.

AUSTIN
Alright, luv! Love it! Turn...pout for me Vanessa. Smashing! Crazy.
Give me some shoulder.
(pause)
Yes! Yes! Yes!
He motions to her two top buttons of her blouse. She nods no. Austin nods yes. She sheepishly undoes them. A MONTAGE of her in various gowns, one more exotic and exciting than the other.

AUSTIN
Show me love. Yes!
(beat)
Smashing!
Vanessa is flanked by two buff MALE MODELS ◈ la Madonna.

AUSTIN
Great! Great! Smashing!
(beat)
Yes! Yes! Yes!
(beat)
No! No!
Love it. Give me love. Give me mouth. Give me lips.

(BEAT)
Going in very close now.
He goes in closer.

AUSTIN
Give me eyes.
(closer)
Give me cornea.
(closer)
Give me aqueous humour.
(closer)
Coming in closer. Give me retina,
Vanessa.
(closer)

Even closer. Give me optic nerve.
(beat)
Love it!
(beat)
And...done.
He throws the camera down.

AUSTIN
I'm spent. What say you we go out on the town?

EXT. LAS VEGAS STREET - BUS - NIGHT
Austin and Vanessa are on the top deck of an open air double- decker English bus having a full-course formal dinner.
They're drinking champagne.
Austin is cutting sausages into ever-smaller pieces, holding his cutlery very English. He has cut one piece to the point to which it's a speck. H puts it on the fork and offers it to her.

AUSTIN
Fancy a nibble?

VANESSA
I couldn't have another bite.
They laugh. They drink. It's TOM JONES, serenading them.
They begin to dance.
Austin gives her roses. Austin is wooing her.

EXT. LAS VEGAS STREET - NIGHT
They walk along the brightly-lit streets, laughing, enjoying each other's company. Austin gives Vanessa a pet rock. She graciously accepts.

64 LAS VEGAS - SUPERIMPOSITION MONTAGE
Austin and Vanessa stroll against a changing series of backgrounds&emdash; neon signs, Vegas icons, dice showgirls, etc.

INT. HOTEL ROOM
Sounds of MOANS and GROANS. We see Austin's backside sticking out above a piece of furniture, then Vanessa's high-heeled leg straining upwards.

VANESSA (O.S.)
Watch out, you're on my hair!

AUSTIN (O.S.)
Sorry. Move your hand to the left.

There you go. Gorgeous.

VANESSA (O.S.)
Go! Just go!
We hear a SPINNING SOUND.

AUSTIN (O.S.)
Left hand, blue.
We now see that Austin and Vanessa are playing TWISTER. She reaches for left hand blue
and they fall over, laughing.

AUSTIN
Wait a tick, I forgot something in the lobby.
(moving behind the couch)
I know what. I'll take the stairs.
Behind the couch, Austin mimes going down stairs.

AUSTIN
Maybe I'll take the escalator.
Austin mimes the smooth descent of an escalator.

AUSTIN
Why take the escalator when I could take a canoe?
Austin mimes rowing a canoe behind the couch.

VANESSA
I haven't had fun like that since college.

AUSTIN
I'm sorry.

VANESSA
Why?

AUSTIN
I'm sorry that bug up your ass had to die.
She laughs too much, making a SNORTING sound.

VANESSA
Always wanting to have fun, that's you in a nutshell.

AUSTIN
No, this is me in a nutshell.

Austin mimes being trapped in a nutshell.

AUSTIN
Help! I'm in a nutshell! What kind of nut has such a big nutshell? How did I get into this bloody great big nutshell?
Vanessa laughs again, SNORTING, tipsy.

AUSTIN
You're smashed, Vanessa.

VANESSA
I am not.

AUSTIN
Oh, yes you are.

VANESSA
I'm not. I'm the sensible one. I'm always the designated driver.
They are both on the bed. She looks at him. He looks at her. There is an awkward silence. She's about to kiss him, then he pulls away.

AUSTIN
I can't. You're drunk.

VANESSA
It's not that I'm drunk, I'm just beginning to see what my Mum was talking about.
(pause)
What was my mother like back in the Sixties? I'm dying to know.

AUSTIN
(sentimental)
She was very groovy. She was so in love with your Dad. If there was one other cat in this world that could have loved your Mum and treated her as well as you Dad did, it was me. But, unfortunately for yours truly, that train has sailed.
Austin hears SNORING. He looks over and sees Vanessa asleep.
A distinctive PHONE RINGS and a

RED LIGHT FLASHES.
Austin opens one of his funky suitcases to reveal a PICTURE
PHONE. It's Basil Exposition, on an airplane.

BASIL EXPOSITION
(on the picture phone)

Hello, Austin, this is Basil Exposition from British Intelligence.

Thank you for confirming the link between Dr. Evil and Virtucon. Find out what part Virtucon plays in something called Project Vulcan.

I'll need you and Vanessa to get on that immediately.

AUSTIN
Right away, Exposition.

BASIL EXPOSITION
Where is Vanessa, by the way?
Austin looks over at Vanessa's sleeping figure.

AUSTIN
She's working on another lead right now.

BASIL EXPOSITION
Then you'll have to go it alone.
Good luck.

AUSTIN
Thank you, Basil.

BASIL EXPOSITION
Oh, and Austin&emdash;

AUSTIN
(knowing)
Yes?

BASIL EXPOSITION
Let me remind you that because of the unfreezing process you might experience flatulence at moments of extreme relaxation.

AUSTIN
Oh, yes. Thank you.

BASIL EXPOSITION
There's one more thing, Austin.

AUSTIN
Yes?

BASIL EXPOSITION

Be careful.

AUSTIN
Thank you.
Austin looks at Alotta's Virtucon business card.

INT. ALOTTA'S JAPANESE STYLE PENTHOUSE
Austin is in a dark penthouse suite. Austin passes a piece of art that is very suggestive of the female anatomy.

AUSTIN
Paging Dr. Freud.
He goes over to a credenza where there is a briefcase. He opens it.

FULL SCREEN - DOCUMENT
Austin's photographing the dossier with his miniature camera/pendant.

AUSTIN
(photographing)
Give it to me baby. Super.
We now see that the document outlines all of Virtucon's holdings in a flow-chart fashion.

AUSTIN
Pout for me, luv. Smashing. Yes!
Yes! Yes! No! No!
One side of the chart is labeled "Secret Projects." Under that we see "Human Organ Trafficking", "Carrot Top Movie", and in CLOSE-UP&emdash; "Project Vulcan."
We see schematics for some sort of subterranean probe and a cross-section of the earth labeled "Crust, Mantel, Core."

AUSTIN
And I'm spent.
The front door opens. It's Alotta.

AUSTIN
You seem surprised to see me.

ALOTTA
I thought you'd quit while you were ahead.

AUSTIN
What, and watch all my earnings go...
(smug)

Down the toilet?

ALOTTA
What do you want, Mr...Cunningham, was it?

AUSTIN
Call me Ritchie, Miss Fagina. May I call you Alotta...
(pause)
Plcasc?

ALOTTA
You may.

AUSTIN
Your boss, Number Two, I understand that cat's involved in big underground drills.

ALOTTA
Virtucon's main interest is in cable television, but they do have a subterranean construction division, yes. How did you know?

AUSTIN
(smug)
I didn't, baby, you just told me.

ALOTTA
It's for the mining industry, Mr.
Cunningham. We can talk about business later. But first, let me slip into something more comfortable.

AUSTIN
Behave!
MUSIC: "The Look of Love" by SERGIO MENDEZ AND BRAZIL 66
Alotta goes behind a Japanese screen. In silhouette she takes off her clothes and puts on a robe. She opens a pair of sliding doors to reveal an elaborate Japanese bath grotto.

INT. JAPANESE BATH
She slips off her robe, revealing a DR. EVIL LOGO TATTOO on her shoulder, and enters the water.

ALOTTA
Come in.

AUSTIN

I'd rather talk about Number Two.

ALOTTA
Don't you like girls, Mr. Cunningham?
Come in, and I'll show you everything you need to know.
Austin takes off his clothes. He is extremely hairy. He goes in. Alotta produces a soapy sponge and swims over.

ALOTTA
May I wash you?

AUSTIN
Groovy.
She washes his back. Behind his back, she pulls out his wallet and looks through it.
ANGLE ON HIS IDENTIFICATION.
It reads "AUSTIN POWERS, INTERNATIONAL MAN OF MYSTERY."

ANGLE ON HIS VARIOUS CARDS: CHARGEX, PLAYBOY CLUB, ETC.
SHE PUTS HIS WALLET BACK IN HIS TROUSERS.

ALOTTA
In Japan, men come first and women come second.

AUSTIN
Or sometimes not at all.

ALOTTA
Care for some saki?

AUSTIN
Sak-i it to me!
Alotta pours them saki. Alotta unscrews the diamond in her ring. A sign on the inside of her ring reads "Relaxation Pills." She drops two PILLS into his drink.
Austin takes a sip. His eyes glaze over. He's instantly woozy.

ALOTTA
How do you feel, Mr. Cunningham?

AUSTIN
Mmmm...I feel extreme relaxation.
A big BUBBLE comes to the surface, right in front of Austin.

AUSTIN

(reciting poem)
'Pardon me for being rude, It was not me, it was my food.
It just popped up to say hello, and now it's gone back down below.'

ALOTTA
That's very clever. Do you know any other poems?

AUSTIN
(reciting in a lofty tone)
'Milk, milk, lemonade.
Round the corner fudge is made.
Stick your finger in the hole, And out comes a tootsie roll!'

ALOTTA
(genuinely moved)
Thank you, that's beautiful. To your health.

AUSTIN
To my health.

ALOTTA
Kiss me.
They go to kiss. She notices HIS TERRIBLE TEETH, CLOSE-UP.

ALOTTA
Do you mind if I ask you a personal question?

AUSTIN
Is it about my teeth?

ALOTTA
Yes.

AUSTIN
Damn. What exactly do you do at Virtucon?

ALOTTA
I'll tell you all in due time, after we make love. But first, tell me another poem.

AUSTIN
I think it was Wordsworth who penned this little gem: 'Press the button, pull the chain, out comes a chocolate choo-choo train.'

ALOTTA
Oh, you're very clever. Let's make love, you silly, hairy little man.
She glides over to him.

INT. PSYCHEDELIC SCENE BREAK
MUSIC: Psychedelic Wa-wa Pedal Funky Drummer Beat GRAPHIC:
The Party Austin and the go-go girl dance crazily.

INT. DR. EVIL'S PRIVATE QUARTERS - DAY
Dr. Evil, Number Two, and Frau Farbissina sit at the large conference table.

DR. EVIL
Austin Powers is getting too close.
He must be neutralized. Any suggestions?

FRAU FARBISSINA
Ya wohl&emdash; I mean, yes wohl,
Herr Doctor. I have created the ultimate weapon to defeat Austin Powers. Bring on the
Fembots!
MUSIC: Sexy Matt Helm-type theme THREE FEMBOTS enter. They are beautiful buxom
multiracial girl/robots in Sixties clothes and white go-go boots.

DR. EVIL
Breathtaking, Frau. These automated strumpets are the perfect bait for the degenerate
Powers.

FRAU FARBISSINA
These are the latest word in android replicant technology. Lethal, efficient, brutal. And no
man can resist their charms. Send in the soldiers!
SEVEN SOLDIERS come in. They are immediately attracted to the FEMBOTS. They
throw down their guns and come to the girls zombie-like.
When they get within range, guns POP out of the Fembots' bras and begin FIRING, killing
the guards.

DR. EVIL
Quite impressive.

FRAU FARBISSINA
Thank you, Herr Doctor.

DR. EVIL
I like to see girls of that caliber.

By caliber, I mean both the barrel size of their guns and the high quality of their character...Forget it.

SFX: 60'S ELECTRONIC BUZZER
NUMBER TWO
That would be the video feed from Kreplachistan.
Dr. Evil and Number Two watch a large screen. We see stock footage of a Russian warhead. We cut into a close-up of RUSSIAN SOLDIERS being taken prisoner by VIRTUCON SOLDIERS in the front of a military vehicle.

DR. EVIL
Gentlemen, Phase One is complete.
The warhead is ours. Let Phase Two begin! Patch us through to the United Nations security secret meeting room.

INT. UN SECRET MEETING ROOM
REPRESENTATIVES of various countries in their traditional garb around a large UN-style meeting table. The BRITISH are dressed in bowler hats. The AMERICANS all look like JFK.
The CANADIANS are dressed as Mounties. The ARABS are dressed in ceremonial robes, etc.

DR. EVIL
Gentlemen, my name is Dr. Evil.
They all look up at the SCREEN.

DR. EVIL
In a little while, you'll find out that the Kreplachistani warhead has gone missing. Well, it's in safe hands. If you want it back, you'll have to pay me...ONE MILLION DOLLARS!
The UN representatives are confused. Number Two COUGHS.

DR. EVIL
(frustrated)
Sorry. ONE-HUNDRED BILLION DOLLARS!
The representatives ARGUE amongst themselves.

UNITED NATIONS SECRETATY
Gentlemen, silence!
(to Dr. Evil)

NOW, MR. EVIL&EMDASH;
DR. EVIL
(angry)

Doctor Evil! I didn't spend six years in evil medical school to be called 'mister'.

UNITED NATIONS SECRETARY
Excuse me. Dr. Evil, it is the policy of the United Nations not to negotiate with terrorists.

DR. EVIL
Fine, have it your way. Gentlemen, you have five days to come up with one hundred billion dollars. If you fail to do so, we'll set off the warhead and destroy the world.

UNITED NATIONS SECRETARY
You can't destroy the world with a single warhead.

DR. EVIL
Really? So long.
The screen goes BLANK.

DR. EVIL
(to evil associates)
Gentlemen, in exactly five days from now, we will be one-hundred billion dollars richer.
(laughing)
Ha-ha-ha-ha.
(slightly louder)
Ha-ha-ha-ha.

EVIL ASSOCIATES
(laughing with him)
Ha-ha-ha-ha.

DR. EVIL & ASSOCIATES
(LOUDER AND MORE STACCATO)
HA-HA-HA-HA-HA!
(louder again, and even more evil and maniacal)

HA-HA-HA-HA-HA-HA-HA-HA!
(PAUSE)
Ohhhh, ahhhhhh...
(pause, quieter)
Ohhh, hmmmm.
(pause, very quiet) hmn.
There is an uncomfortable pause, because clearly we should have FADED TO BLACK.
The evil associates look around the room, not knowing what to do with themselves.

DR. EVIL

Okay...Well...I think I'm going to watch some TV.

EVIL ASSOCIATES
Okay. Sure.
They exit the frame awkwardly.

INT. BRITISH MAKESHIFT HQ
Austin and Vanessa enter past two BRITISH MILITARY POLICEMAN.
There is a communications center, a makeshift armory, bunks, etc.
We see Basil, dressed as the Vegas-era Elvis.

AUSTIN
Hello, Exposition.

BASIL EXPOSITION
Austin, Vanessa, let me bring you up to speed. Dr. Evil has high-jacked a nuclear warhead from Kreplachistan and is holding the world ransom for one-hundred billion dollars. If the world doesn't pay up in four days, he's threatening to destroy the world.

AUSTIN
Thank you, Exposition. Only two things, scare me, and one is nuclear war.

BASIL EXPOSITION
What's the other?

AUSTIN
Excuse me?

BASIL EXPOSITION
What's the other thing you're scared of?

AUSTIN
Carnies.

BASIL EXPOSITION
What?

AUSTIN
Circus folk.
(shudders)
Nomads, you know. They smell like cabbage.

BASIL EXPOSITION

(suffering him)
Indeed...If we could get back to the business at hand. It's one thing to have a warhead, it's quite another thing to have the missiles to launch it.

AUSTIN
Maybe these photographs are the last piece of that puzzle.
(hands him the photos)
I've uncovered the details on Project Vulcan. It's a new subterranean warhead delivery system.

BASIL EXPOSITION
Good God, and underground missile.
We've long feared such a development.

VANESSA
When did you find that out, Austin?

BASIL EXPOSITION
Austin did some reconnaissance work at Alotta Fagina's penthouse last night.

VANESSA
Oh.

BASIL EXPOSITON
Our next move is to infiltrate Virtucon. Any ideas?

VANESSA
Yes, Virtucon runs a tour of their facilities every hour. I suggest we pose as tourists and do site-level reconnaissance.

BASIL EXPOSITION
Top drawer, Kensington. Oh, Austin,
I want you to meet somebody.
Basil waves to an extremely frail ELDERLY BRITISH LADY.

BASIL EXPOSITION
Austin, this is my mother, Mrs.
Exposition. She's in from Tunbridge Wells in Kent. Can you believe, she's ninety-two years old?
Austin hauls off and PUNCHES the lady in the face.

BASIL EXPOSITION
My God, Austin, what have you done?

AUSTIN
That's not your mother, that's a man!
Austin begins tugging on her hair.

MRS. EXPOSITION
Owww...my hair!

BASIL EXPOSITION
Get away from my mother!

VANESSA
Austin, have you gone mad?
The two guards come over and help Mrs. Exposition to a cot.

MRS. EXPOSITION
(through pain)
Who is that man? Why did he hit me?

BASIL EXPOSIION
Don't worry, mother. Lie down.
Austin, you have a lot of explaining to do.

AUSTIN
I'm sorry, Basil, I thought she was a man.

BASIL EXPOSITION
Damn it, man! You're talking about my mother!

AUSTIN
You must admit, she is rather mannish.
No offense, but if that's a woman, it looks like she's been beaten with an ugly stick.

VANESSA
Really, Austin!

AUSTIN
Look at her hands, baby! Those are carpenter's hands.

BASIL EXPOSITION
All right, Austin, I think you should go.

AUSTIN

I think if everyone were honest, they'd confess that the lady looks exactly like a man in drag.

BASIL EXPOSITION
I'm leaving!
(pause)
Oh, and Austin?

AUSTIN
Yes, Basil?

BASIL EXPOSITION
Be careful.

AUSTIN
Thanks.
Basil escorts his mother out.

VANESSA
Austin, may I have a word with you?

AUSTIN
Of course, luv.

VANESSA
Listen, I know I'm just being neurotic, but I can't shake this suspicious feeling about that Italian secretary, Ms. Fagina. I mean, I don't want to sound paranoid, but I've had some bad relationships in the past, and I have some jealousy issues.
You went to her penthouse. It makes me feel so small to give into these insecurities, but I can't help but feel this weird, irrational, unfocused...well, jealousy. I'm sorry.

AUSTIN
Don't be sorry. You're right to be suspicious. I shagged her. I shagged her rotten.

VANESSA
(stunned)
I can't believe you made love to her just like that. Did you use protection?

AUSTIN
Of course, I had my nine-millimeter automatic.

VANESSA
No, did you use a condom?

AUSTIN

Only sailors use condoms, man.

VANESSA

Not in the Nineties.

AUSTIN

Well they should, filthy beggars, they go from port to port. Alotta meant nothing to me.

VANESSA

(pause)

Well, it means something to me. If you want us to have a relationship, you've got to be a one-woman man.

AUSTIN

It was just a shag, Vanessa. You're everything to me.

VANESSA

You just don't get it, do you, Austin?

Good night. Welcome to the Nineties, you're going to be very lonely.

INT. HOTEL ROOM - NIGHT

MUSIC: "What the World Needs Now" by BURT BACHARACH Austin looks at his address book. ANGLE ON THE PAGE: We see a list of names crossed out, with comments written in beside them. Beside Jimi Hendrix we see

"Deceased, Drugs"; Janis Joplin, "Deceased, Alcohol"; Mama Cass, "Deceased, Ham Sandwich"; Jerry Garcia. "Deceased,

Gratefully"; Jane Fonda, "Square".

Austin looks at his old pair of Sixties-era canvas sneakers.

He picks up his new pair&emdash; REEBOK SHAQ CROSS-TRAINER

PUMPS. He pumps them too much and they explode.

Austin looks out his window at the lonely city below. We see the CDs he's just purchased, including SERGEANT PEPPER'S and BURT BACHARACH'S GREATEST HITS.

Austin goes over to the kitchenette and puts a can of unopened Campbell's Tomato Soup in the microwave and turns it on. It explodes in a shower of sparks and soup.

He puts the CD on a record player and drops the needle. The NOISE is awful.

Austin plays MORTAL COMBAT III. His fighter gets his head ripped off, and blood spews out.

Austin is genuinely frightened by this.

INT. BATHROOM

Austin attempts to use the Water Pik, but the head is too loose and water shoots all around the bathroom.

EXT. CAR - STREETS OF LAS VEGAS - NIGHT
Austin drives alone and sad against the rear-projection of Las Vegas.

INT. CASINO BAR - NIGHT
Austin drinks by himself while a gaggle of EIGHT CONTEMPORARY YOUNG PEOPLE IN LOVE cavort. They look at him like he's a freak.
Austin raises a bottle of ZIMA as if to say "hey, I'm down with that". They shoot him sarcastic peace signs. Austin is pleased.

INT. HOTEL ROOM - DAY
Austin sits watching the TIME-LIFE The Last Thirty Years video on TV. Vanessa enters.

AUSTIN
Hello, luv.

VANESSA
Thirty years of political and social upheaval. The fall of the Berlin wall, a female Prime Minister of England, the abolishment of Apartheid, a fascinating tapestry of human strum und drang.

AUSTIN
Yeah, I can't believe Liberace was gay. Women loved him, man. I didn't see that one coming.

VANESSA
Basil was very concerned to know where you were last night.

AUSTIN
Out and about, doing odds and sods.

VANESSA
I'll tell him. By the way, I've decided we should keep our relationship strictly professional.

INT. THERAPIST'S OFFICE - NEXT DAY
We're in the middle of a group therapy session, containing six or seven FATHERS with their teenage SONS. It is emotionally charged. A lot of pained expressions and coffee in Styrofoam cups.

SON 1
(crying)

I love you, Dad.

DAD 1
I love you, Son.
They hug. Everyone APPLAUDS. We see Dr. Evil and Scott.

THERAPIST
That was great, Mr. Keon, Dave.
Thank you. OK, group, we have two new member. Say hello to Scott and his father, Mr....Ehville?

DR. EVIL
Evil, actually, Doctor Evil.

GROUP
Hello, Dr. Evil. Hello, Scott.

SCOTT EVIL
(into it)
Hello, everybody.

THERAPIST
So, Scott, why don't we start with you. Why are you here?

SCOTT EVIL
Well, it's kind of weird.

THERAPIST
We don't judge here.

SCOTT EVIL
OK. Well, I just really met my Dad for the first time three days ago.
He was partially frozen for thirty years. I never knew him growing up.
He comes back and now he wants me to take over the family business.

THERAPIST
And how do you feel about that?

SCOTT EVIL
I don't wanna take over the family business.

DR. EVIL
But Scott, who's going to take over the world when I die?

SCOTT EVIL
Not me.

THERAPIST
What do you want to do, Scott?

SCOTT EVIL
I don't know. I was thinking, maybe I'd be a vet or something, cause I like animals and stuff.

DR. EVIL
An evil vet?

SCOTT EVIL
No. Maybe, like, work in a petting zoo or something.

DR. EVIL
An evil petting zoo?

SCOTT EVIL
(shouting)
You always do that!
(calm)
Anyways, this is really hard, because, you know, my Dad is really evil.

THERAPIST
We don't label people here, Scott.

SCOTT EVIL
No, he's really evil.

THERAPIST
Scott.

DR. EVIL
No, the boy's right. I really am evil.

THERAPIST
Don't be so hard on yourself. You're here, that's what's important. A journey of a thousand miles begins with one step.

SCOTT EVIL

I just think, like, he hates me. I really think he wants to kill me.

THERAPIST
OK, Scott, no one really wants to
"kill" anyone here. They say it, but they don't mean it.
The group LAUGHS.

DR. EVIL
Actually, the boy's quite astute. I am trying to kill him. My Evil Associates have cautioned against it, so here he is, unfortunately, alive.

THERAPIST
We've heard from Scott, now let's hear from you.

DR. EVIL
The details of my life are quite inconsequential.

THERAPIST
That's not true, Doctor. Please, tell us about your childhood.

GROUP
Yes, of course. Go ahead, etc.

DR. EVIL
Very well, where should I begin? My father was a relentlessly self- improving boulangerie owner from Belgium with low-grade narcolepsy and a penchant for buggery. My mother was a fifteen-year-old French prostitute named Chloe with webbed feet. My father would womanize, he would drink, he would make outrageous claims, like he invented the question mark. Sometimes he would accuse chestnuts of being lazy. A sort of general malaise that only the genius possess and the insane lament. My childhood was typical.
Summers in Rangoon, luge lessons. In the spring we'd make meat helmets. If I was insolent, I was placed in a burlap bag and beaten with reeds. Pretty standard, really. At the age of twelve I received my first scribe. At the age of fifteen, a Zoroastrian named Vilma ritualistically shaved my testicles. There really is nothing like a shawn scrotum. At the age of eighteen, I went off to evil medical school. From there...
ANGLE ON THE THERAPIST AND THE GROUP. They are stunned.

PSYCHEDELC SCENE BREAK
MUSIC: Psychedelic Wa-wa Pedal Funky Drummer Beat TITLE
GRAPHIC: Sock It To Me Austin and the go-go girl dance crazily.

EXT. VIRTUCON HIGH RISE - NEXT MORNING
INT. HALLWAY - VIRTUCON

A TOUR is in progress. Austin, Vanessa, and other TOURISTS ride on an electric tram.

AUSTIN
Since I've been unfrozen, I've had a rancid taste in my mouth. Do you have a piece of gum?

VANESSA
(in her own world)
Do you think she's prettier than I?

AUSTIN
Who?

VANESSA
You know who.

AUSTIN
No! Don't lay your hang-ups on me,
Vanessa. You're being very trippy.

VANESSA
I'm looking at you, and the whole time I can't help thinking you had your willie inside her hootchie-kooch.

AUSTTIN
Well put. Listen love, we can't keep having this fight. I'm an International Man of Mystery. Sometimes in the course of my work to save the world I have to shag some crumpet. It's all part of the job.

TOUR GUIDE
Welcome to Virtucon, the company of the future.
(pointing to large display window)
Virtucon is a leading manufacturer of many items you'll find right in your own home. We make steel, volatile chemicals, petroleum-based products, and we also own the Franklin mint, which makes decorative hand- painted theme plates for collectors.
(holds up plate)
Some plates, like the Gone With The Wind series, have gone up in value as much as two-hundred and forty percent, but, as with any investment, there is some risk involved.
The people on the tour APPLAUD.

TOUR GUIDE
Coming up on the left, we have the Virtucon gift shop, offering a wide range of Virtucon licensed products.

On the right, you'll notice a door that leads to a restricted area.
Only authorized personnel are allowed beyond that point.

INT. VIRTUCON GIFT SHOP AREA

All the tourists head for the gift shop. Austin notices a SEVEN-FOOT-TALL SCIENTIST leaving the "RESTRICTED AREA" with a FOUR-HUNDRED-POUND FEMALE SCIENTIST. They both wear Virtucon coveralls.

AUSTIN

I'll take him, you take her.
The seven-foot-tall male scientist goes to the men's room; the four-hundred-pound woman goes to the ladies room. Austin and Vanessa follow.
We hear from inside either washroom the sound of PEOPLE BEING

KNOCKED OUT.

Austin and Vanessa exit wearing the scientists' coveralls over their clothes. Magically, the coveralls fit perfectly.
They go through the doors into the restricted area.

INT. HALLWAY - RESTRICTED AREA

They approach the security GUARD.

VANESSA

Austin, we don't look anything like our photo badges.

AUSTIN

Don't worry, baby. I picked up a mind control technique during my travels to India. I learned it from my guru, the late Guru Shastri, a chaste man who mysteriously died of a disease that had all the hallmarks of syphilis.
Just watch me. Watch me, now.
They reach the guard.

GUARD

Hi, folks. You're entering a restricted zone. Can I see your security badges?

AUSTIN

Sure.
They flash their security badges to the guard.

ANGLE ON AUSTIN. WE PUSH IN SLOWLY AS AUSTIN CONCENTRATES, RAISING ONE EYEBROW AND THEN THE OTHER, BACK AND FORTH.

MUSIC: Mystical Indian sitar.

AUSTIN
(hypnotist-like)
Everything seems to be in order.

GUARD
(looking at the badges)
Hey, wait a minute&emdash;
ANGLE ON AUSTIN. He redoubles his eye-brow-raising.

GUARD
(trance-like, in Austin's English accent)
Everything seems to be in order.

VANESSA
That's amazing. Let's go!

AUSTIN
Hold on one second.
Austin again does his mind control trick.

AUSTIN
Here, have a piece of gum.

GUARD
(in trace)
Here, have a piece of gum.
He hands Austin a piece of gum.

AUSTIN
Don't mind if I do.

GUARD
(slipping out of trance)
Hey! Wait a minute, that's my last piece of gum.
Austin does his mind-control again.

AUSTIN
No, no, I want you to have it, even if it's my last piece.

GUARD
(trance-like)
No, no, I want you to have it, even if it's my last piece.

AUSTIN
(mind-controlling)
I'm going to go across the street and get you some sherbert.

VANESSA

(irritated)
Austin, we have to go!
Shc pulls him away.

GUARD (O.S.)
(faintly)
I'm going to go across the street and get you some sherbert.
Austin and Vanessa come to a door marked "PROJECT VULCAN -
TOP SECRET." They walk through.

INT. PROJECT VULCAN RESEARCH ROOM
Inside, SCIENTISTS wearing head-to-toe radiation suits surround and inspect a huge
diamond-encrusted drill bit.

SCIENTIST
This is the strongest, sharpest drill bit ever produced by man. It weighs fifteen metric tones
and can bore through a mile-thick bedrock of solid granite in seven seconds.

INT. VIRTUCON GIFT SHOP AREA - TOUR TRAM
A SECURITY GUARD and the tour guide take a head count. They notice Austin and
Vanessa's empty seats on the tram. The guard speaks into his walkie-talkie.

INT. PROJECT VULCAN RESEARCH ROOM
SFX: ALARM GOES OFF
ANNOUNCER
(on PA)
Attention, there are intruders in the complex.
All the radiation suited scientists turn to look at Austin and Vanessa.

SCIENTIST
Get them!
The scientist approach. Austin knocks two of them out cold with judo chops.

AUSTIN
Judo chop! Judo chop!
Vanessa knocks two of them out using roundhouse kicks.

SECURITY GUARDS flood into the room from the hallway. Austin and Vanessa take off through another side door which reads

**"VIRTUCON
STEAMROLLER TESTING FACILITY."
INT. STEAMROLLER TESTING FACILITY**
It is a room the size of a large gymnasium overseen by a large observation booth. Six STEAMROLLER go around a test track very slowly.
Austin and Vanessa hide behind one of the slowly moving steamrollers. Security guards enter the facility and begin fanning out in a search.

AUSTIN
Our only way out of here is to drive out!
They climb up the back of a steamroller, KNOCK OUT the DRIVER, push him off, and assume the controls.

P.A. (O.S.)
There they are!
Two SECURITY GUYS jump on either side of the steamroller.
Vanessa wrestles the machine gun off on and pushes him away.
Austin punches the other one off.

AUSTIN
Hang on! I'm going to floor it!
He engages a lever. It goes only slightly faster.
TWO SECURITY GUARDS jump in front of the steamroller. They are acting like they're frozen, ad if in the headlights of a fast-approaching car.

GUARD
Noooooooooooooo!

AUSTIN
Where did you learn to shoot?

VANESSA
Where did you learn to drive?

ANGLE ON THE GUARDS. ONE OF THE GUYS JUMPS OUT OF THE WAY AS IF "IN THE NICK OF TIME."
The steamroller is now 8 yards away. The other army guy is still frozen in the path of the oncoming steamroller.

GUARD

Nooooooooooooooo!

VANESSA
Austin, watch out!

AUSTIN
(looking around)
Where? Where?

ANGLE ON THE GUARD. HE'S BATHED IN THE HEADLIGHTS OF THE STEAMROLLER, WHICH IS STILL 3 YARDS AWAY.

GUARD
Nooooooooooooooo!

ANGLE ON AUSTIN AND VANESSA. AUSTIN IS FRANTICALLY JERKING
The steering wheel and trying to downshift. SFX: Metal grinds. The shifter breaks off along with a gaggle of wares. He desperately jams on the breaks.

ANGLE ON THE GUARD. HE IS FINALLY RUN OVER BY THE STEAMROLLER. THERE IS AN INORDINATE AMOUNT OF BLOOD AND GUTS.
By now, Austin and Vanessa are right by the door. They run out into the hallway.

INT. HALLWAY
The coast is clear.

VANESSA
Thank God, Austin, we made it.

AUSTIN
Yes, act naturally and we'll split this scene the way we came in,
Vanessa.
From behind, a HAND knocks Vanessa and Austin out. It is Random Task flanked by four SECURITY

GUARDS.
INT. STEAMROLLER TESTING FACILITY
We see the aftermath. Several WORKMEN sweep up the blood and guts with large squeegees and brooms. One of them turns to reveal "Steamroller Accident Response Team" written on his jumpsuit.
Another WORKMAN leans down to the body with a hand broom and dust pail to sweep up blood. ZOOM IN on the steamrolled Army guy's ID tag, which reads "STEVE HARWIN."

EXT. SUBURBAN HOUSE - LOS ANGELES
It is a pleasant, Marcus Welby-like ranch-style house. We hear a PHONE RINGING.

INT. KITCHEN
A pleasant-looking MIDDLE AGED LADY answers the phone.

MIDDLE AGED LADY
Hello?
(pause)
Yes, this is Mrs. Harwin.
(pause)
Yes, I have a son named Steve Harwin.
(pause)
Yes, that's right, he's a henchman in Dr. Evil's Private Army.
(pause)
What? Killed?
(pause)
How?
(pause)
Run over by a steamroller? Oh my God. Thank you for calling.
She HANGS UP. A FOURTEEN-YEAR-OLD enters.

FOURTEEN-YEAR-OLD
Hi Mom! When's Steve coming home?
He said he was going to teach me to play ball.

MRS. HARWIN
Sit down, Billy, I have some bad news. As you know, your brother Steven was a henchman in Dr. Evil's Private Army.

BILLY
Was? What is it, Mom?

MRS. HARWIN
Your brother was run over by a steamroller.

BILLY
A steamroller?
(bursting into tears)
No, not Steve! Since Dad died,
Steve's been like a father to me.

MRS. HARWIN
I'm sorry son. People never think how things affect the family of the henchman.
(hugging him)
I love you, Billy.
(to herself, out loud)
I wonder if we'll be able to receive Steve's henchman's comp.
CAMERA PANS to a high-school photograph of Steve on the wall.

INT. PSYCHEDELIC SCENE BREAK
MUSIC: Psychedelic Wa-wa Pedal Funky Drummer Beat TITLE GRAPHIC: The Pad
Austin and the go-go girl dance crazily.

EXT. VEGAS - HIGHWAY
We see a Virtucon electric minivan humming along.

INT. BACK OF ELECTRIC MINIVAN
Austin and Vanessa are unconscious.

EXT. HIGHWAY
The electric minivan turns onto a dirt road that leads to a boulder.

EXT. DESERT - BOULDER
The boulder lifts up and the minivan drives into it.

INT. UNDERGROUND TUNNEL
The minivan enters a long cylindrical tunnel.

INT. FREIGHT ELEVATOR
The minivan is being lowered on a high-speed elevator.

INT. DR. EVIL'S MAIN CHAMBER
VIRTUCON ARMY MEMBERS keep watch. SCIENTISTS check clipboards.

DR. EVIL
Frau Farbissina, check on our guests.
The electric minivan pulls up right next to the immense table.
All the evil associates are present. Dr. Evil squeezes a tennis ball repeatedly. Frau Farbissina opens the rear hatch of the minivan and pulls out Austin and Vanessa.

DR. EVIL
Welcome to my underground lair, Mr.
Powers. Mrs. Kensington's daughter, how lovely. I believe your name is Vanessa? I'd shake your hands, except for obvious reasons.

VANESSA
I don't understand.

DR. EVIL
My hand, dammit! Look at it!

AUSTIN
What's wrong with your hand?

DR. EVIL
Don't try to suck up to me! It's a little late for that. I'm a freak!
Look at it, it's been rendered useless.
He moves his arm around to show them, but it's virtually normal, just slightly aged.

AUSTIN
I'm sorry, baby, I'm just not grocking your head space.

DR. EVIL
Oh forget it. As a fellow player on the international stage, Mr. Powers,
I'm sure you'll enjoy watching the curtain fall on the third and final act.
A large telescreen comes on, showing the United Nations Secret Meeting Room.

DR. EVIL
Gentlemen, I give you the Vulcan.
He presses a button on his chair panel. A giant canvas falls, unveiling an ultra-high tech
diamond-bladed subterranean bore&emdash; the VULCAN. It is rather phallic.

AUSTIN
(under his breath to Vanessa)
Does that make you horny?

VANESSA
(under her breath)
Not now, Austin.

DR. EVIL
The world's most powerful subterranean drill.

INT. UNITED NATIONS SECRET MEETING ROOM
ON SCREEN: Stock footage of volcanoes erupting and animated charts of magma
squirting through the Earth's layers.

DR. EVIL
(voice over)
So powerful it can penetrate the Earth's crust, delivering a 50 kiloton nuclear warhead into the planet's hot liquid core. Upon detonation, every volcano on the planet will erupt.
The various representatives are ABUZZ. Behind the British delegation sits Basil Exposition. To his right, sits Mrs.
Exposition with a hideous BLACK EYE.

AMERICAN UN REPRESENTATIVE
Why should we pay him the money?
He's only got one warhead and he's going to detonate it deep underground.

BASIL EXPOSITION
(the light shifts towards dramatic as he speaks)
My God, man, don't you understand?
It won't just be active volcanoes, inactive ones will erupt as well.
Seven-eighths of the Earth's land mass will be deluged with hot magma.
Tectonic plates will shift, causing massive earthquakes. Imagine no United Kingdom. Think of it, no cricket, no tea, no freshly toasted crumpets smothered with Devonshire clotted cream, the diving mystery of Stonehenge. Imagine severing forever the continuity of Britannic majesty, the demise of this sceptered isle, this jewel, this England...

BRITISH UN REPRESENTATIVE
Any word from Powers?

BASIL EXPOSITION
(back to normal)
I'm afraid we've lost contact with him.

BRITISH UN REPRESENTATIVE
I see.

UNITED NATIONS SECRETARY
Dr. Evil, it seems we have no choice but to pay your ransom.

INT. DR. EVIL'S MAIN CHAMBER
DR. EVIL
Gentlemen, your deadline is in three hours. You have your instructions.
Good-bye.
The screen goes BLACK.

DR. EVIL
Come join us for dinner, won't you Mr. Powers?

INT. DR. EVIL'S PRIVATE QUARTERS
Austin and Vanessa are seated at a table with Frau. WAITERS serve food.
MUSIC: Sexy Matt Helm-type theme

DR. EVIL
I think you'll enjoy the food. I have the best chef in the world.
His name is Ezekial. He's made of seventy-five percent plastic.
Scott enters.

DR. EVIL
Scott my boy, come here. How was your day?

SCOTT EVIL
Well, me and a buddy went to the video arcade in town and, like, they don't speak English
right, and so my buddy gets into a fight, and he goes
'hey, quit hassling me cause I don't speak French or whatever', and the other guy goes
something in Paris talk, and I go 'um, just back off' and he goes 'get out' and I go 'make
me'.

DR. EVIL
(trying to hide contempt)
Fascinating. What are your plans for this evening?

SCOTT EVIL
Thought I'd stay in. There's a good tittie movie on Skinemax.

DR. EVIL
And that's how you want to live your life, is it?

SCOTT EVIL
Yeah. What?

**ANGLE ON A PANEL OF BUTTONS THAT HAS EVERYONE'S NAMES ON IT.
DR. EVIL'S HAND HOVERS OVER THE** button labeled "SCOTT." Frau Farbissina
slaps his hand away.

DR. EVIL
Scott, I want you to meet Daddy's nemesis, Austin Powers.

SCOTT EVIL
Why are you feeding him? Why don't you just kill him?

DR. EVIL
In due time.

SCOTT EVIL
But what if he escapes? Why don't you just shoot him? What are you waiting for?

DR. EVIL
I have a better idea. I'm going to put him in an easily-escapable situation involving an overly- elaborate and exotic death.

SCOTT EVIL
Why don't you just shoot him now?
Here, I'll get a gun. We'll just shoot him. Bang! Dead. Done.

DR. EVIL
One more peep out of you and you're grounded. Let's begin.
A PRIVATE ARMY SOLDIER grabs Austin and Vanessa. Dr. Evil hits a button. One whole wall slides out to reveal a tank.

DR. EVIL
Mr. Powers, Vanessa, some friends of mine are joining us for dinner.
They're quite delighted you'll be part of the meal.
The soldier takes Austin and Vanessa to the tank and puts them in the dipping mechanism.

AUSTIN
Dr. Evil, do you really expect them to pay?

DR. EVIL
No, Mr. Powers, I expect them to die. Even after they pay me the money, I'm still going to melt all the cities of the world with hot magma.
(to guard)
All right, guard, begin the unnecessarily Slow-Moving Dipping Mechanism.
The guard do so. Austin and Vanessa begin to descend slowly towards the surface of the water.

DR. EVIL
Release the sharks!
(to the room)
All the sharks have had laser beams attached to their heads. I figure every creature deserves a warm meal.

FRAU FARBISSINA
(clearing her throat nervously)

Dr. Evil?

DR. EVIL
Yes, what is it? You're interrupting my moment of triumph.

FRAU FARBISSINA
It's about the sharks. Since you were frozen, they've been placed on the Endangered Species List. We tried to get some, but it will take months to clear up the red tape.

DR. EVIL
(disappointed)
Right.
(to Austin)
Mr. Powers, we're going to lower you in a tank of piranhas with laser beams attached to their heads.
Frau clears her throat again.

DR. EVIL
What is it now?

FRAU FARBISSINA
Well, we experimented with lasers, but you would be surprised at how heavy they are. They actually outweighed the piranha themselves, and the fish, well, they sank to the bottom and died.

DR. EVIL
I have one simple request&emdash; sharks with friggin' laser beams attached to their heads, and it can't be done? Remind me again why I pay you people?
What do we have?

FRAU FARBISSINA
Sea bass.

DR. EVIL
Right.

FRAU FARBISSINA
They're mutated sea bass.

DR. EVIL
Really? Are they ill-tempered?

FRAU FARBISSINA

Please allow me to demonstrate.

Frau Farbissina throws a leg of lamb attached to a rope towards the tank, where the WATER BUBBLES and sea bass arch through the air. The sea bass devour the lamb. She pulls the rope back. The lamb has been eaten to the bare bone.

DR. EVIL
Fine. Whatever. Mutated, ill- tempered sea bass it is.
(to the room)
Come, let's return to dinner. Close the tank.

SCOTT EVIL
Aren't you going to watch them?
They'll get away!

DR. EVIL
No, we'll leave them alone and not actually witness them dying, and we'll just assume it all went to plan.

SCOTT EVIL
I have a gun in my room. Give me five seconds, I'll come back and blow their brains out.

DR. EVIL
No Scott. You just don't get it, do you?
Dr. Evil presses a button; the wall closes back over the tank.

INT. TANK AREA
Austin and Vanessa slowly descend towards the water. They can see the WATER BUBBLING beneath them.

VANESSA
What's your plan?
Just then, a SEA BASS jumps out of the water, just missing Austin.

AUSTIN
First, I plan to soil myself. Then,
I plan to regroup and think about the next move. Any thoughts?

VANESSA
Sadly, no. Hold on! I always keep this on me just in case.
She pulls out a container of dental floss.

AUSTIN

All right, I get it. I have bad teeth. You have to understand, in Britain in the Sixties you could be a sex symbol and still have bad teeth.
It didn't matter.

VANESSA
No, no, no. We'll use the floss to get to the ledge.

AUSTIN
Smashing idea! Give it to me.
Austin takes the container and draws out four feet of dental floss and spins the container above his head like a bolo.
He throws it and it wraps around a RADIATOR and it catches like a grappling hook.
Austin begins drawing out the floss to take up the slack.
Meanwhile, the slow-dipping mechanism is edging towards the sea bass. Unfortunately, Austin is still drawing out the floss. He keeps pulling out floss.
More floss still. The mechanism continues to sink. Finally, the floss line goes TAUT. Austin ties it off high on the pole of the slow-dipping mechanism. Austin holds out his hand like a surgeon&emdash;
Vanessa places a tube of toothpaste in his hand. Meanwhile the guard is reaching to undo the floss. Austin places the open tube on his palm, aimed at the guard. Vanessa WHISTLES at the guard loudly. He turns around.

AUSTIN
Judo chop!
Austin JUDO CHOPS the toothpaste tube, sending a stream of toothpaste into the guard's eyes.

GUARD
(screaming, rubbing his eyes)
My eyes! My eyes!
Austin folds the tube across the top of the wire, grabbing both ends.

AUSTIN
Hold on, Vanessa!
She grabs onto him and they slide down the floss to safety right as the dipping mechanism goes under the water.
Meanwhile, the guard waits for them with toothpaste smeared all over his face.
He and Austin STRUGGLE.
The guard manages to get Austin pinned to the ground, Austin's head dangling over the water. SEA
BASS circle. The water boils, dangerously close to Austin's head.

VANESSA

(shouting)
Austin, watch out!
Austin FLIPS the guard over. The SEA BASS chew the guard's head off like a blender.

AUSTIN
Not a good time to lose one's head.

VANESSA
Indeed.

AUSTIN
That's not the way to get ahead in life.

VANESSA
Yes.

AUSTIN
It's a shame he wasn't more headstrong.

VANESSA
Shut up.

AUSTIN
Fair enough.
They head out a door. ANGLE ON THE HEADLESS TORSO. The name tag reads "JOHN SMITH."

EXT. HOOTERS RESTAURANT - DAY
It is a sports bar-type restaurant that has scantily clad

BUSTY WAITRESSES.
INT. HOOTERS RESTAURANT
At a table we see fifteen or so TWENTY-SOMETHING GUYS, scouting chicks, drinking mugs of beer.

GUY 1
I can't believe John Smith is getting married tomorrow.

GUY 2
Where is Smittie anyways? It's not like him to be late for anything, especially his own stag party.

GUY 3

Well, you know he's a henchman for Dr. Evil. Sometimes they work late.
Can I just say something that may sound a little sappy? I think it's a testament to our friend John that so many of his buddies showed up in his honor. There's a lot of love in this room.
A large-breasted WAITRESS approaches with a phone.

WAITRESS
Hi, I have a phone call here for the John Smith party.

GUY 1
Hello?
(pause)
Yes, I have a friend named John Smith.
(pause)
That's right, he's in Dr. Evil's private army.
(pause)
What? He's dead?
(pause)
Decapitated by mutated flying sea bass? Oh my God! OK, thank you.
He hangs up.

GUY 2
(to Guy 1)
Hey Bill, what's wrong? Was that John? Is he coming late?

GUY 1
Guys, John's not coming.

GUY 2
Why?

GUY 1
He was decapitated by mutated flying sea bass.

GUYS
(upset)
Oh no, oh my God, etc.

GUY 1
All right, to Smittie!
Everyone raises their glasses.

GUYS
To Smittie!

INT. PSYCHEDELIC SCENE BREAK
MUSIC: Psychedelic Wa-wa Pedal Funky Drummer Beat TITLE
GRAPHIC: Out of Sight Austin and the go-go girl dance crazily.

INT. CORRIDOR
Austin and Vanessa drive a Dr. Evil golf cart down a brightly- lit, narrow corridor to a doorway marked "Emergency Exit."

VANESSA
What do we do now?

AUSTIN
We've got a freaked out square and world annihilation is his bag. You go get help. I'm gonna stay here and keep an eye on the bad Doctor.

VANESSA
I'm not going anywhere. We're a team.

AUSTIN
Too right, youth. That's why I need you to lead the troops.

VANESSA
I'll hurry back.

AUSTIN
Listen, Vanessa, whatever happens, I just want you to know that I feel bad about shagging that Italian girl.
I had a sip of sake and all of the sudden, I don't know what happened.
The whole time I was shagging her&emdash; I mean really shagging her, I mean it was crazy, I was like a huge mechanical piston, in and out, IN and OUT!&emdash;

VANESSA
(cutting him off)
Austin, what's your point?

AUSTIN
Anyways, what I'm trying to say is that if you want me to be a one-woman man, well, that's just groovy, because...I love you.

VANESSA
Oh, behave!
Vanessa goes out the door.

INT. LADDER
Vanessa starts climbing up the ladder.

INT. CORRIDOR
Austin tries to turn the cart around in the narrow corridor.
He begins a twenty-seven point turn.

INT. DR. EVIL'S PRIVATE QUARTERS
Dr. Evil, Scott and the evil associates finish dinner.

DR. EVIL
Come, everyone, let us repair to the main chamber. Project Vulcan is about to begin. Scott, are you coming?

SCOTT EVIL
I don't want to.

DR. EVIL
Don't you want to see what Daddy does for a living?

SCOTT EVIL
(under his breath)
Blow me.

DR. EVIL
What did you say?

SCOTT EVIL
Show me.
They all go towards a giant door with the radiation symbol painted on it.

INT. CORRIDOR
Austin's still trying to turn the cart around. PULL BACK TO
REVEAL&emdash; The cart is completely wedged perpendicularly in the corridor. Austin jumps out and starts running down the hall. Austin comes to a T in the hall and goes around the corner. He sees two GUARDS and ducks into a door.

INT. FEMBOT LAIR
Inside are SEVEN FEMBOTS lounging in various seductive poses on Sixties furniture&emdash; egg chairs, trapezes, round furry bed, etc.
MUSIC: Sexy Matt Helm-type theme

AUSTIN
Hello, hello.

FEMBOT
Hello, Mr. Powers, care to have a little fun?

AUSTIN
(looking at his watch)
No, actually, I have to save the world.
He runs towards to door to exit. Suddenly, A PAIR OF FEMALE
LEGS drop and wrap around Austin's neck and lift him up.
His feet leave the floor.
Another FEMBOT cartwheels up to Austin. Nozzles pop out of the tips of the Fembot's
bra.

AUSTIN
Is it cold in here?
A cloud of multicolored gas spews from the nozzles. Austin is overcome. The room starts
to spin.

INT. DR. EVIL'S MAIN CHAMBER - CONTROL AREA
Dr. Evil sits into his chair with his radiation suit on.

DR. EVIL
Arm the probe!
A small electric flatbed comes in carrying the nuclear warhead. A PHALANX of Dr. Evil's
soldiers run beside it.
The cart approaches the subterranean probe and the warhead is loaded up into its tail.

INT. FEMBOT'S LAIR
Austin is on the bed being held down by the Fembots.
Psychedelic music plays. Projected colored swirling lights flash. The Fembots swirl around
seductively.

AUSTIN
(delirious)
I've got to get Dr. Evil!
(eyes closed, fingers in his ears)
Margaret Thatcher naked on a cold day! Margaret Thatcher naked on a cold day! Margaret
Thatcher naked on a cold day!

INT. DR. EVIL'S MAIN CHAMBER
The (very phallic) Vulcan droops to its down position.

DR. EVIL
Probe in place.
TECHNICIANS in "VIRTUCON" lab coats scurry about, being technical.

DR. EVIL
Five minutes to go. Let the penetration countdown begin.
Dr. Evil presses a button marked "PENETRATION BEGIN." Next to it is a large button that says "ABORT." ANGLE ON AN
EASTERN EUROPEAN TECHNICIAN at a microphone.

EASTERN EUROPEAN TECHNICIAN
(on PA, very slowly, with very thick accent)
Five minutes and COUN-ting.

EXT. DESERT
Vanessa leads fifteen COMMANDOS on ATCs across the sand.

INT. FEMBOT LAIR
Two Fembots guard the door and five are on the bed in come- hither poses.

FEMBOT
You can't resist us, Mr. Powers.
Eventually you'll give in.

AUSTIN
Au contraire, I think you can't resist me.
MUSIC: Sexy Matt Helm-type theme Austin starts his seductive dance. He does a quick head count of the Fembots, reaches out of frame, pulls out eight cigarettes, put them in his mouth and lights them with a blowtorch.
He throws seven cigarettes one by one. Each cigarette lands perfectly in a different Fembot's mouth. Austin smokes the remaining cigarette.
Austin begins to do a seductive striptease. The Fembots are aroused. He takes off his shirt, revealing his hairy chest, and focuses his sexual energy on one Fembot.
She begins to shake violently, her head shaking back and forth like in Jacob's Ladder.
Eventually her head explodes. Austin is now stripped down to his Union Jack bikini briefs and turns to another Fembot. Her head explodes.
He takes off his shoes and throws them away cavalierly.
Then he tosses down his lit cigarette and grinds it with his bare foot. He gives a look of disguised pain.
He mouths "I love you" to another Fembot. Her head explodes.
He does the 'I'll call you' hand signal to yet another Fembot, whose head explodes.
Austin does a hip-thrust to another and her head explodes.

Austin leans over and wags his rump to the two remaining Fembots.

AUSITN
Oh, I fell over.
Their heads explode simultaneously. All the Fembots are lying on the floor, smoking. Just then, Vanessa enters, flanked by a COUPLE OF COMMANDOS. She surveys the scene and looks at Austin in his briefs. She's hurt. The commandos salute Austin.

AUSTIN
It's not what it looks like, Vanessa.
(to the commandos)
At ease, boys.

VANESSA
(glancing down)
Likewise.

AUSTIN
I can explain. They attacked me.
Gas came out of her...well, and then they...and I...

VANESSA
I believe you, Austin. Let's go.

AUSTIN
Hold on a tick, let me put on my togs.

INT. MAIN CHAMBER
Austin and Vanessa lead FIFTEEN COMMANDOS into the chamber and GUNFIRE breaks out. Two CATWALKS run the length of the chamber, meeting at the door to the control area.
The commandos split into two groups and lob grenades at the PRIVATE ARMY SOLDIERS who are guarding the stairs leading to the catwalks. They go flying.

INT. CONTROL AREA
The ALARM goes off.

DR. EVIL
Activate the blast shutters!
Metal shutters automatically cover the windows overlooking the probe mechanism.

DR. EVIL
Launch the subterranean probe!

The giant probe engine begins to throb and whirl. The tip of the spinning probe suddenly strikes the floor of the chamber and burrows into the earth with atomic force. Smoke and debris explode upwards. The entire chamber quakes violently&emdash; eight on the Richter scale.

EASTERN EUROPEAN TECHNICIAN
We have penetration. Subterranean detonation&emdash; two minutes and COUN-ting.

INT. DR. EVIL'S MAIN CHAMBER
Austin, Vanessa, and three commandos are pinned down behind several VIRTUCON BARRELS

INT. CATWALK
Another FOUR GUARDS block their way. Austin goes to shoot, but he's out of bullets.

SFX: CLICKA-CLICKA
Austin and Vanessa run along the catwalk towards the control room.
They're directly in the path of TEN

CHARGING PRIVATE ARMY SOLDIERS.
AUSTIN
Follow me! We're going to have to jump over the rail!

VANESSA
Are you crazy?

AUSTIN
Don't worry!

ANGLE ON SIDE SHOT OF CATWALK
They continue to run towards the guards behind some STACKED
BARRELS. Two OBVIOUS STUNT DOUBLES run out from behind the barrels in a continuous motion instead of Austin and Vanessa and diver over the rail.

ANGLE ON THE OTHER TEAM OF COMMANDOS
They are making progress on the other catwalk.

ANGLE ON AUSTIN AND VANESSA
They have landed safely, but are surrounded by FIVE PRIVATE
ARMY SOLDIERS, armed to the teeth&emdash; one has a bazooka, one has a flamethrower, one has a Gatling gun, etc. They see Austin and throw down their weapons, pulling out KNIVES.
One of the private soldiers runs at Austin and he stabs him.

Another soldier runs at Austin, and Austin also stabs him.
A third private army soldier runs at Austin. Austin does the stabbing motion.

SFX: CLICKA-CLICKA
AUSTIN
Blast! Out of ammo.
Vanessa unleashes a series of kicks, knocking them all out.

INT. CONTROL ROOM
Austin begins to enter.

VANESSA
Austin, I'm coming with you.

AUSTIN
I'm going it alone this time, Vanessa.
I have a follow-up visit with the Evil Doctor.

VANESSA
I'll secure the perimeter.

INT. CONTROL AREA
Austin enters the control area. A VIRTUCON ARMY MAN fires at him. Austin returns fires, shooting up some electrical equipment. Live wires dangle dangerously. Austin sees Mr.
Bigglesworth running out a read door.

DR. EVIL (O.S.)
Come, Mr. Bigglesworth!
Austin heads for the door until he smacks into AN INVISIBLE
FORCE FIELD. He turns and sees a bank of old-fashioned computers labeled "DESTRUCTACON 5000".

DESTRUCTACON (V.O.)
Good afternoon, Mr. Powers, I'm the Destructacon 5000. I'm programmed to prevent you from progressing beyond this point. You might as well surrender. Resistance is futile.
Your odds of survival are 23,763,273 to

AUSTIN
Well, Destructacon 5000, you have quite a head on your shoulders, I dare to coin.

DESTRUCTACON (V.O.)
Yes, I am programmed to answer any question.

AUSTIN
Really? Let me ask you this. What is love?

DESTRUCTACON (V.O.)
That does not compute.

AUSTIN
Why not? It's a question.

DESTRUCTACON (V.O.)
Love is...love is...love is...
The computers begin to smoke. Alarm bells ring.

DESTRUCTACON (V.O.)
Remjack! Remjack!
(singing)
Daisy, Daisy...
(faster)
Remjackremjackremjack!
There is a muffled explosion. The computer goes dark. Austin passes through the force field and heads for the door until he hears&emdash;

EASTERN EUROPEAN MAN
(on PA)
Subterranean detonation&emdash; one minute and COUN-ting.
He begins looking furiously for the abort button.

AUSTIN
(to Eastern European Man)
Where's the abort button?
The Eastern European Man holds up his finger as if to say
'give me one second.'

EASTERN EUROPEAN MEAN
(on PA)
Forty-five seconds and COUN-ting.
(to Austin)
It's right over there.
Austin sees the abort button. It is across the room. Just then, Random Task enters. Austin sees him and goes to shoot him, but he has run out of bullets. Random task takes off his SHOE.
Austin makes his way across the room to the button.

Random Task THROWS HIS SHOE.

ANGLE ON SHOE SPINNING IN THE AIR
The shoe HITS AUSTIN IN THE HEAD. Austin pauses. The shoe has not killed him. It has just hurt him slightly.

AUSTIN
Ow! That really hurt. I'm going to have a lump there, you idiot! Who throws a shoe? You fight like a woman.

EASTERN EUROPEAN MAN
(on PA)
Fifteen seconds and COUN-ting.
Random task blocks Austin's way to the button. He stands there, menacing, missing one shoe.
Exposed wires are everywhere. On the counter beside Austin is a Big Gulp.

AUSTIN
Care for a drink?
Austin throws the drink at Random Task's feet. It lands in front of him on a pile of exposed wires. Electricity travels through the Big Gulp, up Random Task's wet sock, ELECTROCUTING him.
He begins to SMOKE, and then dies.

AUSTIN
Shocking.

EASTERN EUROPEAN MAN
Three...two...one...
A 50 kiloton explosion from deep in the earth rocks the control area.

EXT. STOCK FOOTAGE MONTAGE - VOLCANOS ERUPTING
Different volcanoes around the world. Lava spews and flows.

INT. CONTROL AREA
Austin dives in SLOW MOTION towards the abort button. He flies through the air for an inordinate length of time.

AUSTIN
(slow motion distortion)
Nooooooo!
His hand lands on the button.

EASTERN EUROPEAN MAN
(on PA)
Abort.

EXT. STOCK FOOTAGE MONTAGE - REVERSE VOLCANO ERUPTIONS
Lava, smoke and debris sucks back into volcanoes around the world. (Eruption footage run in reverse.)

INT. CONTROL ROOM
Having saved the world, Austin picks up a MACHIEN GUN from a fallen Private Army guy and runs to the door at the back, chasing Dr. Evil.

INT. CORRIDOR
Austin chases after Dr. Evil.

INT. DR. EVIL'S PRIVATE QUARTERS
Austin bursts in, catching Dr. Evil packing a suitcase.

AUSTIN
I've got you, Dr. Evil!

DR. EVIL
Well done, Mr. Powers. We're not so different, you and I. It's true, you're British, and I'm Belgian.
You have a full head of hair, mine is slightly receding. You're thin,
I'm about forty pounds overweight.
OK, we are different, I'm not making a very good point. However, isn't it ironic, Mr. Powers, that the very things you stand for&emdash; swinging, free love, parties, distrust of authority- are all now, in the Nineties, considered to be...evil? Maybe we have more in common than you care to admit.

AUSTIN
No, man, what we swingers were rebelling against were uptight squares like you, whose bag was money and world domination. We were innocent, man. If we'd known the consequences of our sexual liberation, we would have done things differently, but the spirit would have remained the same. It's freedom, man.

DR. EVIL
Your freedom has cause more pain and suffering in the world than any plan I ever dreamed of. Face it, freedom failed.

AUSTIN

90

That's why right now is a very groovy time, man. We still have freedom, but we also have responsibility.

DR. EVIL
Really, there's nothing more pathetic than an aging hipster.
Alotta enters. She holds a gun to Vanessa's head.

ALOTTA
Not so fast.

DR. EVIL
Well, it seems the tables have turned,
Mr. Powers.
Just then, Scott Evil enters.

SCOTT EVIL
Hey, Dad, I can take my Sega, right?
Austin grabs Scott and puts the gun to his head.

AUSTIN
It seems the tables have turned again,
Dr. Evil.

DR. EVIL
Not really. Kill the little bastard.
See what I care.

AUSTIN
Man, you are one chilly square!

SCOTT EVIL
Dad, we just made a breakthrough in group!

DR. EVIL
I had the group liquidated, you little shit. They were insolent.

SCOTT EVIL
I hate you! I hate you! I wish I was never artificially created in a lab.

DR. EVIL
Scott, don't say that...

Scott runs off. In the confusion, Vanessa KNOCKS the gun out of Alotta's hands. Alotta pulls out a knife. Austin SHOOTS the knife out of her hand. Vanessa grabs Alotta by the throat.

VANESSA
This is for sleeping with my man, you whore!

ALOTTA
I didn't sleep with him.

VANESSA
I don't believe you.

ALOTTA
(choking)
It's the teeth.

VANESSA
OK, I believe you. But you still must be chopped.
Vanessa gives her a judo chop.

VANESSA
Judo chop!
Meanwhile, Dr. Evil has run to the egg shaped rocket, which closes and begins to lift up through

A HOLE IN THE CEILING. HE RUNS IN. ON THE WAY, HE FLIPS A SWITCH WHICH SAYS "SELF-DESTRUCT - 5:00 MINUTES."
EASTERN EUROPEAN MAN (O.S.)
(on PA)
Five minutes to self-destruct and COUN-ting.
Austin SHOOTS and misses. Rocket exhaust pours out of the hole in the ceiling.

AUSTIN
Let's split!
Austin and Vanessa run out the door into the...

INT. CORRIDOR
They pass Number Two, who is front of an open safe, stuffing his pockets with cash while the others are trying to escape.
Austin and Vanessa run to the main chamber...

INT. MAIN CHAMBER

...to the main corridor...

INT. MAIN CORRIDOR
...past the Fembot lair, over the wedged-in cart, to the escape ladder. They begin to climb.

INT. MAIN CHAMBER
Explosions, debris, the cavern begins to collapse.

134 STOCK FOOTAGE - DESERT FLOOR - MERCURY TEST SIGHT
Ground caving in from an underground nuclear explosion.

EXT. RAFT - MIDDLE OF THE OCEAN - DAY
Austin and Vanessa are floating in a large inflatable raft.
FIERY DEBRIS falls in the water around them.

VANESSA
I have something to tell you.

AUSTIN
Lay it on me.

VANESSA
I love you, Austin.

AUSTIN
That's fab, because I love you, too,
Vanessa.

VANESSA
Kiss me.

AUSTIN
Behave!
Austin and Vanessa draw towards each other, preparing for a passionate kiss. Just as their lips are about to touch, however, they are interrupted by a strong WIND and the noise of a HELICOPTER OVERHEAD. Their hair is blown all about and the waves are whipped into a frenzy.

AUSTIN
Just when things were getting interesting.

ANGLE ON BASIL EXPOSITION WEARING SCUBA GEAR, BEING LOWERED ON A ROPE FROM THE HELICOPTER. HE STOPS JUST ABOVE THEM.

BASIL EXPOSITION
Well, Austin, you've stopped Dr.
Evil from destroying the world with his subterranean nuclear probe, and somehow you and
Agent Kensington managed to escape unscathed from his evil lair.

AUSTIN
I'd say that about sums it up,
Exposition.

BASIL EXPOSITION
Not quite, actually. Vanessa, I have something for you.
Basil hands Vanessa an official-looking set of leather-bound credentials.

BASIL EXPOSITION
Because of your exemplary service to Her Majesty, you are now officially an active Field
Agent with all the privileges and responsibilities thereof.

VANESSA
Thank you, Exposition. I'm honored.

AUSTIN
Congratulations, Field Agent Kensington!

BASIL EXPOSITION
Austin, I have something for you as well.
He hands him a business card.

BASIL EXPOSITION
Here's the number of my dentist, he's first rate. Ring him up, he'll look after you.

AUSTIN
Thanks, Basil. Maybe the Nineties aren't so bad after all.

VANESSA
Oh, Austin.
Austin and Vanessa embrace and kiss.

BASIL EXPOSITION
Austin, now, about your next mission&emdash; Still kissing Vanessa,
Austin motions with his thumbs to the pilot of the helicopter to lift Basil up. He rises away
in mid- sentence.

BASIL EXPOSITION
(rising up)
But, wait, I&emdash; you got me again.
Oh, and Austin&emdash;

AUSTIN
(calling out)
Yes Basil?

BASIL EXPOSITION
(rising)
Be careful!
Austin and Vanessa kiss again. The helicopter blows them around. The CAMERA TILTS UP to the sky and continues to rise, until we are in&emdash;

EXT. SPACE
We see DR. EVIL'S CAPSULE in orbit around the Earth.

DR. EVIL (V.O.)
I'll get you yet, Austin Powers!

END CREDITS ROLL
LAST CREDIT reads "SEE AUSTIN POWERS IN YOU ONLY FLOSS ONCE."

AUSTIN POWERS LOGO
ANNOUNCER (V.O.)
Now you can get all the Austin Powers movies in one Laser Disk box set!
Virtucon Home Video presents "The Powers Collection."

DISPLAY TABLE
With five laser Disks laid out, alongside a PK-47, Austin's glasses, and floss and a toothbrush.

ANNOUNCER (V.O.)
Relive all your favorite Austin Powers movies, including...

141 GRAINY, BLACK & WHITE CLIP
Showing Mike as Austin Powers, with Fifties hair and suit, against a rear projection of explosions and stunts from stock footage.

ANNOUNCER (V.O.)
Middle Name: Danger.

AUSTIN
So, Dr. Evil, do you expect the world to pay the ransom?

DR. EVIL
No, Mr. Powers, I expect them to die.

ANNOUNCER (V.O.)
No Austin Powers collection would be complete without some of the later hits, like...

SEVENTIES FILM CLIP
ANNOUNCER (V.O.)
Four Eyes Only.
We see Austin from behind, talking to a GIRL in a bathing suit.

GIRL IN BATHING SUIT
Oh, Austin, kiss me.
He turns around. It's Austin Powers, played by ROGER MOORE, with the same glasses and bad teeth.

ROGER MOORE
Oh, behave!
He does a frightening grin, displaying the AWFUL TEETH.

ANNOUNCER (V.O.)
We've also included some of the more obscure hits, like...

143 VERY RUNNY COLOR FILM CLIP
ANNOUNCER (V.O.)
From India With Affection.
We see Austin Powers played by an INDIAN GENTLEMEN, same glasses, same bad teeth.

INDIAN AUSITN
(Indian accent)
Well, my good fellow, are you expecting me to pay the ransom to you, you despot?

INDIAN DR. EVIL
(Indian accent)
No kind sir, I expect you to go up in the evolutionary chain. But first,
I expect you to sing.

INDIAN AUSTIN
(singing, Indian atonal)

'IF MUSIC BE THE FOOD OF LOVE, LET'S BAKE A CAKE.'
DISPLAY TABLE
ANNOUNCER (V.O.)
All the Austin Powers adventures in one Laser Disk boxed set!

145 CLIPS FROM MOVIE - AUSTIN IN TIGHT CLOSE-UP
AUSTIN
Behave!

THE END

Made in the USA
Middletown, DE
27 August 2021